Action Research for
Professional Development

Concise advice for new (and experienced)
action researchers

Jean McNiff

September Books
Dorset

© Jean McNiff 2010

First published 2010
by September Books
24 Highland Road, Poole, Dorset
BH14 0DX

Reprinted 2011, 2013

British Library Cataloguing in Publication Data
A catalogue record for this book is available from the British Library.

ISBN 978-1-902047-03-4

Printed in Great Britain by Berforts Information Press Ltd.

Contents

Acknowledgements

I wish to thank all those who have contributed to the book and helped me develop my thinking and writing along the way.

Thank you especially to the following people who read the manuscript in whole or in part, and for the wonderful conversations and happy times.

Jenny Carpenter
Mark Cordery
Maria James
Clare McCluskey
Peter McDonnell
Keither Parker
Julie Pearson
Peter Raymond
Jane Renowden
Alex Sinclair
Val Stephenson
Jack Whitehead
Jill Munro Wickham

I will both lay me down in peace, and sleep; for thou, Lord, only makest me dwell in safety.
(Psalm 4: 8)

If I take the wings of the morning, and dwell in the uttermost
parts of the sea;
Even there shall thy hand lead me, and thy right hand shall hold me.

... when I awake, I am still with thee.
(Psalm 139: 9, 10, 18)

INTRODUCTION

This book is an easy guide to action research. It is intended for new action researchers, though I hope experienced action researchers will find it useful too. Although it is written in an accessible style, the ideas are the ones you would find in most scholarly journals, and the coverage of topics is comprehensive and set out in a systematic way.

The book is an upgrade on the booklet *Action Research for Professional Development* to be found at http://www.jeanmcniff.com/ar-booklet.asp. This booklet continues to be used world-wide on work-based and higher degree professional education programmes, and for the time being it will remain on the website for anyone who wishes to access it, download it, photocopy it, and use it in any way they see fit.

The present book has been written in response to many requests for an equally easy book that also has greater coverage and more in-depth discussion of some of the key issues. Many readers have also requested examples of ideas in practice, and exercises they can use for themselves or with their students. So in each chapter you will find topics for discussion, examples, and reflective questions to get you thinking further. In this sense, it is a workbook as well as a textbook.

You will note the particular focus on work-based learning, since this is a core feature of professional development programmes in continuing and higher education. You will also see that the book is made relevant to practitioners across the professions, to reflect the growing take-up of action research in nursing and health care, business and management, teaching, and the public services. It also reflects the international reach of action research: most of the stories in the examples are drawn from my own experiences with colleagues around the world.

I hope you enjoy the book. It was written with joy, and I hope this is your experience in reading it. Please let me know if it can be improved in any way.

You can contact me at jeanmcniff@mac.com. I will respond, perhaps not immediately, but I will.

Jean McNiff
Dorset, September 2010

PART ONE

ALL ABOUT ACTION RESEARCH

This part deals with practical issues in action research. It contains Chapters 1, 2, 3, 4, 5 and 6.

Chapter 1 asks, 'What is action research?' It gives a summary of the key features of action research.

Chapter 2 asks, 'Why do action research?', and explains how doing action research can enhance your professionalism.

Chapter 3 asks, 'Who can do action research?', and responds that all practitioners are able to do it.

Chapter 4 asks, 'What is involved in doing action research?', and gives a brief outline of the main issues involved.

Chapter 5 asks, 'How is action research different from traditional research?', and gives succinct explanations of the differences.

Chapter 6 gives a summary of the main features of action research.

Each chapter links ideas about doing action research and improving professionalism through knowledge creation. The point is made throughout that each practitioner can and should hold themselves accountable for what they do.

Chapter 1
What is action research?

This chapter sets out some main ideas about action research. It engages with the following questions:

- What is action research?
- What does this involve?
- What does this mean in practical terms?

WHAT IS ACTION RESEARCH?

Action research is a practical way of looking at your work in any profession to check that it is as you would like it to be. If you feel that is already good quality, you describe and explain what you are doing to other people and say why you think they should agree with what you are saying. If you feel that your work could be better, you find ways to improve it.

Because action research is done by you, the practitioner, it is often referred to as practitioner research, or practice-based research; and because it involves you in thinking about and reflecting on your work, it also becomes a kind of self-reflective practice.

The idea of self-reflection is central. In traditional forms of research – for example, in disciplines such as sociology, psychology or management – researchers tend to do research on other people. They observe others and ask, 'What are they doing? How can their actions be described and explained?'

In action research, people observe and do research on themselves. They ask, 'What am I doing? How can my actions be described and explained?'

In traditional research, researchers enquire into other people's lives; they do research *on* other people. Action researchers enquire into their own lives; they do research *with* other people. This makes action research a democratic and inclusional practice. Action research becomes an enquiry by the self into the self, though it is always done in company with other people.

WHAT DOES THIS INVOLVE?

Action research involves finding ways to improve your practice and then explaining how and why you have done so. You ask, 'How do I improve my practice?' (Whitehead 1989). If you decide that something needs improving, or investigating further, you take action to improve it. You then stand back and consider whether you have achieved what you set out to achieve. If you have, you tell your peers what you have done, to see if they agree with what you are claiming. If not, you go back and try other ways until you are reasonably confident that things are better.

WHAT DOES THIS MEAN IN PRACTICAL TERMS?

In practical terms, this means that you, a practitioner, think about your own life and work, which involves asking yourself why you do the things you do, and why you are the way you are. This makes you a practitioner-researcher.

It also means you can show how you have carried out a systematic investigation into your practice, and can offer descriptions and explanations for what you are doing and why you are doing it that way. Ideally, you can explain how you have a better understanding of yourself, and how you intend to continue developing yourself and your work. On the other hand, you may find areas where things are not going as you wish, in which case you take steps to improve what you are doing, and offer explanations for what you have done and why you have done it.

Action research therefore becomes a kind of self-evaluation. It lets you take control of your own practice and make judgements about its quality. You act, reflect on, and make judgements about what you are doing. If you feel your work is already the best it can be, you produce evidence to explain why you feel this way. If you feel it could be better, you do something about it so that it does come up to standard. This point is especially important if you are doing action research in an organisational setting.

A useful way of thinking about action research is that it is a strategy that helps you to live in the way you feel is a good way. It helps you to live out the things you believe in (your values); and it enables you to give good reasons every step of the way.

EXAMPLES

Here are some examples of the things different kinds of researchers are interested in, and the kinds of questions they might ask.

Traditional researchers are interested in knowing how and why things work as they do. For example:

> Ron is a dentist. He wants to know if there is a connection between brushing your teeth regularly and keeping them healthy. He asks, 'How can I show the connection between brushing your teeth and keeping them healthy?'

> Emad is a teacher. He believes there is a relationship between caring teacher-student relationships and the quality of learning in his classroom. He asks, 'What is the connection between the quality of teacher-student relationships and the quality of learning?'

Traditional researchers tend to see issues 'out there'. They investigate the issues from a values-neutral perspective, while aiming to demonstrate a cause and effect relationship between variables.

Action researchers are interested in taking action to improve things. For example:

> Sue is also a dentist. She wants to know how she can persuade children to brush their teeth regularly. She asks, 'How can I persuade children to brush their teeth regularly?'

> Hessa is also a teacher. She also believes that there is a relationship between the quality of teacher-student relationships and the quality of learning. She asks action research questions, such as, 'How do I help students learn better through developing caring student-teacher relationships?'

Action researchers always see themselves as associated with the issue they are interested in. They investigate the issue from a values-committed perspective, and they check their findings against the critical feedback of others. Their work is always linked with their values, and they make judgements about their work in relation to how well they realise these values in practice.

EXERCISE

Please do the following exercise. You could do it with a friend, or by yourself, using your reflective journal. (Your journal can be a beautifully expensive book or a systematic collection of papers, or even take the form of a series of e-mails or messages to friends on Twitter. Do whatever is right for you to keep a record of what you are thinking.)

- Think of any work-based issue that you are interested in to do with your work. Do you want to raise standards? Do you want to improve something? Do you want to help someone?

- Draw a picture of the 'thing' that you are interested in. Now draw a picture of yourself (perhaps draw a stick figure) and the issue you wish to investigate.

- Think – Where do you position yourself? Are you standing outside the issue, observing it but not doing anything about it? Or do you see yourself as part of it, influencing it?

Doing this exercise will help you decide whether you wish to do traditional research, where you investigate something 'out there'; or whether you wish to do action research, where you investigate something near to your heart with a view to taking action to improve the situation.

REFLECTIVE QUESTIONS

Ask yourself these questions:

✓ Do you see the relevance of action research for your practice?
✓ Do you want to evaluate your work? Why?
✓ Can you see how your practice is linked with your values? How?
✓ What do you want to find out? Why?
✓ Do you see any challenges ahead?

SUMMARY

This chapter has looked at some of the key issues in action research. Specifically, it has made the following points:

- Action research is practice-based. These practices communicate the values that inspire your work and life.

- It involves reflecting on and evaluating your own practice and taking action to improve any unsatisfactory elements.

- It is different from traditional forms of research, where researchers tend to do research on other people. Instead, action researchers do research on themselves in company with other people.

Now let's look at Chapter 2, which gives reasons why you should do action research.

Chapter 2

Why do action research? You and your professional development

This chapter enables you to give explanations for why you are doing action research, in the form of the reasons and purposes for what you do, and why you should see yourself as a competent practitioner and a professional. It contains these sections.

- You as a professional
- How can doing your action research help your professionalism?
- So, what do you need to know?

YOU AS A PROFESSIONAL

As a professional you should be able to say, 'I am good at my job.' If you say this, you can expect people to say, 'Prove it.' Your response is, 'I can't "prove" it, but I can produce reasonable evidence to show that what I am saying is true and I am not making it up.' It is then your responsibility to produce the evidence to back up your claim.

Producing evidence is an aspect of doing research. This is why it is important to do research into your own practice in order to produce the evidence, and not stay at the level of making unsubstantiated claims.

Professionalism is therefore a matter of both (1) being able to say that you are good at your job and (2) doing research to produce evidence to back up your claims that you are good at your job. You are able to say that your practice is research-based and evidence-based. This also enables you to show how you are accountable to others and yourself.

HOW CAN DOING ACTION RESEARCH HELP YOUR PROFESSIONALISM?

Let's look at what is involved in being a professional and how doing action research can help.

What is involved in being a professional?	What is involved in doing action research?
A professional is able to say what they are doing and why they are doing it.	Action research is a process of describing what you are doing and explaining why you are doing it.
A professional can genuinely say that they know what they are doing.	Action research, like all kinds of research, is about producing knowledge. In your case, it is about producing knowledge of your practice.
A professional can produce evidence to back up their knowledge claim.	Through investigating your practice, you are able to generate evidence to back up your claim that you know what you are doing and why you are doing it.
A professional is ready to describe and explain what they are doing, to show how they hold themselves accountable for their work.	Action research is a process of offering descriptions and explanations for what you are doing, to show how you hold yourself accountable for your work.
A professional is able to say how and why they can improve any aspect of their work.	Action research enables you to investigate any aspect of your work, say why it is an important aspect, and explain how you intend to improve it.
A professional is able to take charge of their own practice and say how they intend to develop it.	Doing action research enables you to take charge of your own practice; you become your own professional developer.
A professional engages in collegial practices and checks their ideas with others.	You check your provisional ideas against the critical feedback of your colleagues to ensure you are staying on the right track.

Also …

Professionalism is judged in terms of whether the practitioner can show that they care for their clients, have a clear sense of what they are doing, and demonstrate their competence in all areas.	You can explain how and why you care for your clients and how you have developed a clear sense of what you are doing. You can demonstrate your competence in all areas.
A practitioner can raise their status as a professional by explaining what they are doing and why they are doing it. If they cannot do this, they raise doubts about their credibility as professionals.	Action research is a process of offering descriptions and explanations for what you are doing and why you are doing it. By creating a research base for your practice, you establish your credibility firmly in the eyes of your clients and peers.
A professional can identify career development pathways.	Action research can enable you to profile your development and explain what your capabilities are, for example, when applying for a new job.

SO, WHAT DO YOU NEED TO KNOW?

You need to know that action research is about

Taking action

This is about what you do and how you are trying to improve it. It means finding better ways of doing things – and …

Doing research

This is about how you give descriptions and explanations for what you are doing and how you are trying to improve it, and why it is important that you improve it.

Both aspects are equally important, and always go together.

Action research is therefore both about taking action to improve something in your practice, and also about researching the action, which means investigating what you are doing and offering descriptions and explanations for why you are doing it. This contributes to your professionalism. Being a professional means explaining that you know why you are doing what you are doing, and can give a justification and a rationale for it in the interests of accountability.

EXAMPLES

John is an architect. He keeps records of his meetings with clients, and his correspondence with them. He can show that he has responded to all their requests about the layout of their houses, and that he has taken into consideration their wishes to change the layout or re-arrange rooms to their satisfaction. He can claim to be demonstrating respect for his clients.

Úna is a social worker. She can produce records to show that she visited families on a regular basis, and according to an agreed schedule. She can claim to be fulfilling her duty of care to her clients.

Both can claim these aspects of their professionalism by producing the evidence that they are doing their jobs well.

EXERCISE

Talk with a critical friend about the following questions. (A critical friend is someone who listens carefully to what you are saying, and gives you critical but supportive feedback.)

- How do I understand my professionalism?
- How can I show that I am a professional?
- What are my responsibilities as a professional?
- Am I accountable? For what? To whom?
- How can I improve what I am doing?

REFLECTIVE QUESTIONS

Ask yourself:

✓ Are you completely satisfied with what you are doing in your workplace?

✓ Do you want to change anything? If so, what?

✓ How do you think things could be better?

✓ Do you want to do something about it? What?

✓ Will you encounter any barriers to change? If so, what do you think they will be? Will you be able to do something about them?

SUMMARY

This chapter has given reasons why you should do your action research, specifically:

- Doing action research into your own practice can enable you to enhance your professionalism.

- You are able to provide an evidence base to show that you are demonstrating the hallmarks of a professional.

- You do action research to enable you to give explanations for what you are doing as a professional.

This raises the question, 'Who can do action research?', which is the focus of the next chapter.

Chapter 3
Who can do action research?

This chapter deals with issues about who can do action research and especially whether practitioners can be researchers. It asks these questions.

- Who can do action research?
- What are the links between taking action and doing research?
- What does this mean for your work-based learning?

WHO CAN DO ACTION RESEARCH?

You can. I can. Potentially we all can.

It is not particularly difficult to do action research. Think about any event when you had no idea how to do something, yet you found out through tackling it in a systematic way. Take the example of riding your bike. How many tries did it take before you stopped falling off your bike and actually rode it? The chances are that you did not stop after each fall and rationalise why you were falling off. You probably just tried out new strategies until you were successful. (Or perhaps your mum kept running down the road holding on to your seat – you are never alone in life, and especially not when you do action research.)

You were going through the key methodological steps of action research because you

- identified an issue,
- imagined ways of tackling it,
- tried out a possible strategy for improvement,
- evaluated the situation,
- and changed your thinking and practice in light of the evaluation.

Your focus was on improving your capacity to act in a right way – in this case riding your bike. This is the basis of professionalism. You improve your capacity for right action by first improving your learning about what you should do.

WHAT ARE THE LINKS BETWEEN TAKING ACTION AND DOING RESEARCH?

However, taking action is not the same as doing research, because research is always about creating knowledge and giving explanations for how you have done so; and professionalism is not only about taking the right action, but also explaining why you took that action.

So in action research you

1. take action to improve something;
2. make sure you understand what you have done;
3. use that new understanding (knowledge) to give explanations for how and why you have improved it (in academic terms, this means that you generate new theory – the word 'theory' means 'explanation').

Turning a story of action into a research account

Let's look at what it would take to turn your story of learning how to ride your bike into a research account. Here is how you can do it.

*   You say first that you wanted to learn how to ride your bike;
*   say why it was important for you to do so;
*   gather data (e.g. photos, e-mails) about how you were riding it initially (when you were falling off);
*   describe what you did to improve (so that you stayed on); and
*   describe what the situation turned into (a successful bike ride).
*   Continue gathering data to show the processes of learning to ride your bike;
*   find pieces of data to back up your claim when you say, 'I can now ride my bike, and I know how I have learned to do it';
*   explain the significance of all these processes to other people, including your peers, and invite their critical feedback;
*   and ride off to work on your bike.

EXAMPLE

Here is an example of how you can turn this into a research story to tell your colleagues. The example takes the form of an e-mail to your friend George.

Dear George,

Here is a nice story that I think you will enjoy. It is about how I have learned how to ride a bike.

I decided to learn how to ride a bike because I was concerned about how much petrol I was using by driving my car. It was a concern because I am aware that excessive fuel emissions are damaging our environment, and I wanted to do whatever I could to conserve energy and save the planet. I wanted to turn this project into a research project for a module on my professional development course, so I decided to gather data from the start.

First I decided to keep my reflective journal: you can read my entry of 21.2.10 where I wrote: 'I cannot ride my bike. I keep falling off.' I also sent e-mails to friends telling them about my decision to learn to ride a bike – see my e-mails of 3.2.10 to Laura; and of 10.2.10 to Mike. I have copies of the dated e-mails in my data archive on my computer. Learning how to ride my bike therefore became the focus of my action enquiry.

At first I could not manage to ride my bike, so I took the advice of two critical friends and did the following: I put stabilisers on my rear wheels, and I visualised myself riding my bike along a straight line. I still kept falling off, but less often. I got Susie, my sister, to observe me and record the number of times I fell off, so that I had a record of achievement over time. Eventually I got to the point where I could stay on for a whole minute! What an achievement! Soon I was riding round in circles, and I even got Susie to take a photo of me standing up on the pedals as I rode. I am now a successful bike rider, without stabilisers, and I have a whole data archive of photos, e-mails, text messages, observation schedules, and my journal to show the process of my learning and my actions.

I think learning how to ride my bike is significant for me – and other people – because I am now actually conserving energy and contributing to saving the planet. I can produce key pieces of data as evidence to show that I am telling the truth and not making this up – look at the photo of me standing on the pedals! I am also getting very healthy with all this exercise. Now I must stop as I am going to work – on my bike!

Yours,

Jo

WHAT DOES THIS MEAN FOR YOUR WORK-BASED LEARNING?

The upshot is that you can improve your professionalism by doing action research. You focus first on improving what you are doing. You then make your account public, and explain the significance of what you are doing, so that others can see the evidence base of your claims to professionalism, and check that you are telling a true story. This means they can have confidence in your capacity to produce good quality practice and also to demonstrate the integrity of what you say.

Most professionals aim to improve their practice all the time. For many, this is a condition of professional registration. Even the best (perhaps especially the best) continue to practise; even Olympic champions, the world's best, continue to try to improve.

So who can do action research?

These ideas are important when responding to the question 'Who can do action research?' In traditional views, it is mainly academic specialists in higher education who are able or qualified to do research and to produce knowledge, i.e. say they know something that was not known before. This is not necessarily the case.

Practitioners in every workplace context can also do research and produce knowledge. You can research your own practice in the following fields, and thousands more: dentistry, sales, mountaineering, shopkeeping, advertising, housekeeping, gardening, manufacturing, administration, medicine, accountancy, writing … and any other form of work you can think of.

The point is that you can

- show how you are able to improve what you are doing, and
- produce descriptions and explanations for what you are doing, to back up your claim that you know what you are doing.

Doing this positions you as a researcher. You do not need someone else to offer explanations for your personal or professional life. You have accepted the responsibility of doing it for yourself and you have decided to show how you hold yourself accountable for what you are doing to the wider world.

Further, by producing your account of practice, you are showing other people how they can do the same thing, so you are influencing their learning, and possibly also their sense of wellbeing in their own professionalism.

EXERCISE

Think of any issue you are interested in. Think of how you can take action to improve it. For example:

- You want to learn to type using all your fingers, in order to save time.

- You are concerned that you are wasting time by watching too much television.

Now map out how you could do something about it, using the same plan as above.

Write an e-mail to a friend, telling the story of what you have done – again, as above.

By doing this you are actually writing an action research account. With some editing it could go into a professional portfolio, or become part of a course for accreditation.

REFLECTIVE QUESTIONS

Think about these things:

✓ What issue is interesting you at the moment?

✓ Do you see how you could take action to tackle it?

✓ How do you think you can monitor what you are doing and gather data about it?

✓ Could you turn it into a formal action enquiry?

SUMMARY

This chapter has considered the question of who is able to do action research. It has made the following points.

- All practitioners can do action research.

- They tell their stories of action within an explanatory frame.

- By doing action research, you position yourself as a professional who is able to show the research base of your practice.

The next chapter tells you about what is involved in doing action research, and should help you deepen your insights into the processes.

Chapter 4
What is involved in doing action research?

This section explains what is involved in doing action research, which means

- taking action to improve practice;
- explaining what you have done and creating knowledge; and so
- generating theory – read this section if you are on an accredited course to help you to explain why you are doing action research, or if you want to learn more about the field.

TAKING ACTION TO IMPROVE PRACTICE

We have seen from previous sections that improving practice involves these steps.

- You look at what you are doing;
- Consider if it is satisfactory, or needs improving somehow;
- Decide to do something about any aspects you feel need attention;
- Try out new ways of working;
- Think about how these might be better than before;
- Continue working in this way if they are better; or try something different if they are not.

These are common-sense steps that most people do (or think they do) all the time when they are at work. They are action steps (not research steps) that aim to improve practice.

Now let's consider more carefully how you can develop a research perspective, and turn 'ordinary' action into research-based action. Doing this will also enable you to say that you are creating new knowledge.

EXPLAINING WHAT YOU HAVE DONE AND CREATING KNOWLEDGE

Doing action research involves these steps:

- You identify an issue that you wish to investigate, and say why it is an issue for you;

- Formulate a research question, about 'I wonder what would happen if …?' or 'How do I find ways of doing this?' or 'How do I improve what I am doing?';

- Monitor what is happening and gather data about it;

- Say how you are going to make judgements about progress (identify criteria that indicate good quality);

- Generate evidence from the data to test the validity of any emergent claims that you have found ways of dealing with the issue;

- Change practice and thinking in light of your evaluation.

Doing action research can therefore be seen as about monitoring and recording what you are doing so that you can explain the steps you have taken to other people. Your explanation is about your knowledge and practice. You can say, 'I know what I am doing, and I can produce the evidence to show that this is the case.' Because it is about how you are improving what you are doing in professional contexts, you can say, 'I have improved my work and I can explain to you how and why I have done so.'

In other words, doing research involves looking at what you are doing both from an action perspective and also from a research perspective.

The different perspectives involve slightly different kinds of language, as follows.

Action perspective	Research perspective
I want to improve something	I identify a research issue
I can say why I want to improve it	I can explain why I want to research this
I need to see what the situation is like at the moment	I gather data to show what the situation is like at the moment
I imagine how I can do something to improve things	I look at my data to help me imagine ways of improving the situation
I try out new ways of working	I take action to see if I can improve the situation
I check with other people about what I am doing	I test my provisional conclusions against the critical feedback of others
I say why what I am doing is important	I explain the significance of the actions I have taken and their effects
I keep working in this way if things are satisfactory, or do something else if not	I modify my ideas and actions in light of my evaluation

Improving practice and doing research therefore merge. You see things both from an action perspective and also from a research perspective. The action is about doing, while the research is about saying how you know what you are doing.

Saying that you know something is called a claim to knowledge, or a knowledge claim. Your knowledge claim is that you know

- what you are doing
- how you are doing it

- why you are doing it (your reasons) and what you hope to achieve (your purposes)

- the significance of what you are doing, probably in relation to the positive influence it is having on your own and other people's learning.

Being able to say that you know all these things enables you to claim that you are a practitioner-researcher, and that your practice is highly professional practice.

Examples of knowledge claims

Here are some examples of knowledge claims:

- I am a farmer. I know how to look after animals and I know why I need to do so.

- I am in sales. I know what customers want, how I can sell it to them, and why I should take certain actions and not others.

- I am a sailor on a cruise ship. I know how to sail ships, and I also know how to look after customers. In both cases I can say why I need to know these things.

Examples of action research leading to knowledge claims

Tom works at a zoo. He explains how he tries to improve the quality of life for animals, what he does, and why he does it. He can explain how he is contributing to the welfare of the animals.

Pam is a higher education tutor. She can explain what she does as she supervises trainee teachers, and how and why she does it. She appreciates how she is potentially influencing students' learning, as well as her own.

Sameera is a teacher. She can explain what she is doing as a teacher, and she knows why she is doing it. She can say why she does her job and how it gives meaning to her life.

Now let's consider how action research can help you generate new theory.

GENERATING NEW THEORY

(Read this section if you are on a higher degree programme, or if you would like to learn more about action research at a deeper level.)

When you explain what you are doing, you offer a theory of practice. The word 'theory' means 'an explanation'. Theories come in the form of existing knowledge, and also new knowledge that you create. For example, you might say, 'I have a theory about how keys and locks work', which means 'I can explain how keys and locks work, and why they work as they do.' This is part of your existing knowledge. When you undertake your action enquiry, you aim to generate new knowledge about your practice. You offer descriptions and explanations for what you are doing. This is new knowledge and new theory. Your theory of practice enables you to explain what you are doing, and how and why you are doing it. As a professional, therefore, you can offer your own personal theory of practice: you can theorise what you are doing. This kind of theory tends to be called 'living theory' because it lives in the life of the practitioner who is taking the action.

Steps involved in generating a personal living theory of practice

You may find it helpful to think of how the following steps can help you to generate your personal living theory of practice.

- You observe what you are doing, and check whether everything is satisfactory.

- You describe what you are doing, and gather data to show your situation as it is.

- You take action to improve any aspects that need attention. You keep careful records of what you are doing.

- You explain what you are doing in terms of your reasons and purposes (why you are doing it, and what you hope to achieve). These reasons and purposes are often linked to your values. Values are the things that give meaning to your life, such as love or kindness or professional excellence. We all try to live our values in our practices in some way – that is, we try to live out what we believe in.

- You articulate the significance of what you are doing, in terms of the importance it has for your own life and possibly the lives of other people.

- You say how you intend to continue to improve what you are doing, or develop your present ways of working.

You can now say that you have theorised your practice; i.e. you can offer an explanation for what you are doing and why you are doing it.

EXAMPLE

Joe is a chef. He wants to find ways of turning his restaurant into the best in the region. He is inspired by his wish to be excellent in everything he does. He decides to do this as an informal action enquiry.

He begins by taking stock of his products – menus, recipes, seating arrangements in the restaurant. He draws up a list of excellent and not so excellent points. He gathers data in the form of customers' evaluations, numbers of customers on different days of the week, amount of food returned uneaten on plates. He decides to introduce a special cuisine of Mediterranean food at weekends, with a traditional budget menu during the week.

He monitors the same indicators over time. He sees that more people begin to visit at weekends, which indicates improved customer satisfaction. He experiments further with the dishes, fulfilling his own desires for culinary excellence. He judges the improvement in his practice by the number of customers coming through the door, which in turn is an indication of his wish to celebrate his excellence and turn his restaurant into the best in the region.

He is able to report to the environmental health officers who regularly visit to monitor the state of kitchens and restaurant that he engages in his own regular self-evaluation. They are pleased with the rigour of his evaluation and award him a special Certificate of Excellence, which he reproduces in the local newspaper as a special advertising feature for his restaurant.

EXERCISE

Talk with a critical friend about these questions.

- Do you agree with Joe's strategies? Could he do anything further? What lessons can be drawn from his story?
- Is there any aspect of your practice that you think you could improve? If so, what? What could you do?
- How do you think you can realise your own standards of excellence in your job?
- Anything else?

REFLECTIVE QUESTIONS

Think about these things.

- ✓ Is it important to improve your own practice? Why?
- ✓ What might happen to your workplace if you do? What might happen if you don't?
- ✓ What might happen to you? What might happen to others?
- ✓ Anything else?

SUMMARY

This chapter has dealt with the following points.

- Doing action research usually follows a systematic process of action-reflection steps.

- You can develop a research perspective to the actions you take: this can turn your action into research-based action.

- You can generate your own living theory through studying your practice and analysing and explaining it in a systematic way.

In the next chapter we consider how action research lends itself to ongoing professional development, and specifically how it is different from traditional forms of research.

Chapter 5
How is action research different from traditional research?

This chapter sets out how action research is different from traditional research. It will help you to explain why you have chosen to do action research.

The chapter addresses the questions:

- How is action research different from traditional research?
- What are the main differences between action research and traditional research?
- When would you use different research methodologies?

HOW IS ACTION RESEARCH DIFFERENT FROM TRADITIONAL RESEARCH?

Action research is different from traditional research in a range of ways, and there are differences of opinion about how and why they are different. Here are some things that traditional researchers and action researchers tend to think about their different kinds of research.

What traditional researchers and action researchers tend to think about their different kinds of research

What traditional researchers tend to think	What action researchers tend to think
Only academic practitioners can do research and generate knowledge	All practitioners can do research and generate knowledge.

Practitioners have to be told what to do and think about their practice.	Practitioners can think for themselves and make their own decisions about practice.
Knowledge is a thing that exists in someone's head (usually an academic's).	Knowledge is a creative process that all people engage in, intellectually and physically.
There is an answer to everything, and it can be discovered somewhere.	There is no final answer to anything. Knowledge can be created as well as discovered.
All research will lead to an end point.	There are no end points in life or human enquiry, only continual processes of new beginnings.

Action researchers believe that all people can do research, because

- Everyone can produce evidence to show that they know what they are doing;

- They can say how they have come to know this;

- They can explain its importance for their own new learning, and possibly the new learning of other people.

WHAT ARE THE MAIN DIFFERENCES BETWEEN ACTION RESEARCH AND TRADITIONAL RESEARCH?

The main differences between action research and traditional research about these issues are:

- Who studies what
- How they study it
- Why they study it and what they do with their findings.

Who studies what

What traditional researchers tend to study	What action researchers tend to study
Traditional researchers study the world 'out there', from an outsider perspective. They ask, 'What is going on over there?'	Action researchers study the world 'in here', from an insider perspective. They ask, 'What is going on in here?'
They study other people, seeing those people as separate from themselves.	They study themselves, seeing themselves as connected with everyone and everything else. The 'I' studies the 'I' in company with other people.
They offer explanations for what other people are doing, but remain separate from the people they are studying.	They offer descriptions and explanations for what they are doing in company with other people.

How they study it

How traditional researchers tend to study	How action researchers tend to study
Traditional researchers tend to carry out experiments on things and people, using traditional scientific methodologies, including quantitative data gathering and statistical analysis.	Action researchers investigate their own practices together with the people they are with, starting from where they are. They offer explanations for how they think and act, and how they are trying to improve things. They often use qualitative forms of data gathering and analysis, though they frequently use quantitative forms too.
They often use control and experimental groups.	They produce their written and visual narratives to show their work in action.

They tend to say, 'If I do this, that will happen', aiming to show a cause-and-effect relationship between what they do and what other people do.	They do not say, 'I caused this to happen.' Instead they say, 'I had an influence somewhere.'

Why they study it and what they do with their findings

Why traditional researchers study and what they do with their findings	Why action researchers study and what they do with their findings
Traditional researchers want to find out facts and measurements about the external world.	Action researchers want to find out how they can improve the world, starting with themselves.
They do this so that they can make recommendations about how events can be predicted and managed.	They take responsibility for what they are doing, and encourage others to do the same.
They publish their work in scientific books and papers, usually as printed texts. Their findings tend to take the form of abstract theories which they expect other people to apply to their own practices.	They publish their living theories of practice in books and papers, often as visual texts, to influence the development of new open forms of thinking and practices that carry hope for the future.

WHEN WOULD YOU USE DIFFERENT RESEARCH METHODOLOGIES?

You would use traditional research methodologies when –

- You want to find out how many people do different things. You ask, 'How many people use this supermarket?', and you count the number of people who go in and out.

- You want to see the effect of fertiliser on your flowers. You can compare growth in an experimental group and in a control group.

- You want to find out whether Brand X washing powder is better than Brand Y. You test one batch of washing, using Brand X, against another batch using Brand Y, and compare the results in terms of cleanliness.

You would use action research methodologies when –

- You want to find ways of improving practice. You ask, 'How do I improve what I am doing?'

- You want to work with other people and inspire them to ask the same kind of question.

- You want to give an account of what you are doing.

EXAMPLE

Karin is a doctor. She is committed to the idea of patient care. She sees the best form of patient care in prescribing the most appropriate medicines. She is involved in a large-scale experiment to see whether a new drug will contribute to a cure for illness. The experiment involves administering the drug to a certain group of people, to see if there is a direct relationship between the drug and recovery from illness. A placebo is given to a control group of people.

Roula is also a doctor. She is also committed to the idea of patient care. She sees the best form of patient care in talking with patients and caring for their emotional needs as well as prescribing the best medicines and caring for their physiological needs. She asks, 'How do I help patients help themselves?' She encourages her patients to say, 'I know how to help myself, and I can do it.' She sees this as the first and most important step in their recovery.

EXERCISE

Talk with your critical friend about how you would find out about the following: this means deciding which methodologies you would use.

- You are going on holiday and you want to find out which is the cleanest beach in the area.

- You want to find ways of improving relationships in your organisation.

- Your present washing up liquid does not clean as well as you wish. How do you decide which could be a better one?

- You want to get to know the pretty lady on the bus. How do you do this?

REFLECTIVE QUESTIONS

Ask yourself:

✓ Why do you want to use action research? When is it more appropriate than traditional research? In what way?

✓ Why is it important to know the difference?

✓ Would it make a big difference if you didn't use action research? What may be the potential risks if you do? Or if you didn't?

SUMMARY

This chapter has set out the main differences between traditional research and action research. These differences are as follows.

- Traditional researchers and action researchers hold different assumptions about what people know and how they come to know it.

- The main differences lie in assumptions about who studies what, how they study it, and why they study it.

Knowing what these differences are will help you decide which methodology to choose and to justify your choice.

The next chapter gives a summary of the main features of action research.

Chapter 6
A summary of the main features of action research

This chapter sets out the main features of action research, saying what it is and what it is not. It also makes the point that different kinds of research are not necessarily incompatible.

The section contains these points.

- What are the main features of action research?
- What are the most effective ways of understanding the processes involved?
- How can different methodologies work together?

WHAT ARE THE MAIN FEATURES OF ACTION RESEARCH?

Before we begin, it is worth bearing in mind that 'action research' is not a 'thing' in itself, but a form of words that describes what you as an action researcher do. Action researchers are real-life people who wish to investigate their practices and offer explanations for what they are doing so they can show how they hold themselves publicly accountable. The term 'action research' refers to real people who are evaluating their practice with a view to improving it.

Here is a summary of the main features of action research, and also a summary of what it is not.

What action research is ...

The main features of action research

- Action research is practice based. It is done by people who see themselves as practitioner-researchers who want to find out more about their practices with a view to improving them.

- It is about learning, and using that learning to improve practice. It is not about manipulating behaviours through specific interventions.

- It is about creating knowledge, usually about what you and other people are doing. This means that what is common knowledge today may change by tomorrow.

- It is values laden. Practitioners identify what gives meaning to their lives (their values) and try to find ways to live these values better in their practices.

- It is educational, which means that people are encouraged to find ways to think for themselves and then encourage others to do so too.

- It is collaborative. Practitioner researchers appreciate that they are always in company with others, horizontally in current time and space, and vertically through time and influence.

- It is critical and risky. Improving one's thinking in order to improve one's practices involves questioning what we think is the case, and possibly changing our positions in light of greater honesty. This can be uncomfortable, and often requires considerable courage.

- It is always political. The aim of action research is always to improve practice through improving learning, and using that learning through words and living example to influence others to develop more just and equitable organisational and social practices.

... and what action research is not

Here are some of the things that action research is not

- Action research is not scientific research, which claims to be value-free, and focuses on establishing cause and effect relationships. However, action research is always systematic and methodologically rigorous.

- It is not only about doing projects within a bounded time, though you may do projects if you wish. It is more about adopting an enquiring attitude to life, and backing up any knowledge claims with authenticated evidence.

- It is not comparative research, where you compare one group with another; or longitudinal research, where you track changes over time. It is about starting from where you are and tracking changes in your own and others' learning and action as you proceed.

- It does not aim to accept or refute a given hypothesis. The starting point is to look at what you know and what you are doing, and ask, 'Does this need improving? How do I improve it? Do I need to change what I know and do, and develop new knowledge and new ways of acting?'

- It does not look for concrete answers. Action researchers tend to be comfortable with uncertainty and the unpredictable nature of life.

- It is not necessarily the most appropriate methodology. Sometimes other kinds of research are more appropriate for finding out what you need to know: for example, how many people use a particular kind of milk.

Remember – No research methodology can provide all the answers. When you research your own work, you may find that you stop looking for answers and focus instead on asking interesting questions. The point is not to look for a happy ending or solution, because there is no such thing. Life is ongoing, and the end of one thing becomes the starting point for another. The aim is always to find ways of making life more interesting, meaningful and fulfilling.

WHAT ARE THE MOST EFFECTIVE WAYS OF UNDERSTANDING THE PROCESSES INVOLVED?

One of the most effective ways of understanding something is to visualise it. Try using visualisation to help you understand how to choose and use different research methodologies. Here are some ideas to help you.

Traditional research tends to follow a linear pattern, with a clear beginning (usually a hypothesis) and a definitive end point: something like this.

$$A \rightarrow b \rightarrow c \rightarrow d \rightarrow ... n$$

When you do traditional research, you may feel that you begin at a specific starting point and work your way towards an answer at the end.

BEGINNING ————————> THE END

Action research, on the other hand, tends to follow a dynamic pattern of generative transformational iterations, where one point acts as the beginning of new points, in a self-perpetuating spiral (see Figure 12.1, p.72).

When you do action research, you may feel that you begin at a point that is a continuation of what was happening before, and you now try out different pathways. There is no 'correct' way, and you will not know which is the right one until you are on it.

What action research is and is not, and how it should be represented, forms part of contemporary debates.

HOW CAN DIFFERENT METHODOLOGIES WORK TOGETHER?

Although they use different approaches, and are underpinned by different assumptions, traditional research and action research often work in close harmony. Action researchers often draw on the ideas of traditional researchers to help them clarify their starting point, or to decide how to gather, analyse and use data. Here is an example of how this can be done.

EXAMPLE

Mohammed and Sana work together for a railway company. They both want to find ways of attracting customers to use their service. They reason that a key way of doing this is to ensure customer comfort.

Sana is a traditional researcher. She decides to test her hypothesis that people generally prefer travelling from Birmingham to London by train. She does this by carrying out surveys and interviews with commuters. She analyses the results statistically, and comes up with strong evidence that leads her to conclude that train is most people's favourite form of transport for this particular journey.

Mohammed is an action researcher. His job is to find ways of ensuring that people using the train service have the most comfortable journey possible from Birmingham to London. Using Sana's findings, he begins designing new forms of seats and seating plans for trains that will ensure customers' comfort. He begins by asking himself, 'I wonder how I can produce a really comfortable seat for people who are travelling long distances?', and he starts producing and trying out new designs.

EXERCISE

Using the ideas in this section, try the following.

Working with a critical friend, draw your own visual representation of how you understand action research. Check with your friend to see if they can relate to your model, and use it to make sense of their own work. Invite them to show you their model, and see if you can relate to it too.

Draw a picture of yourself doing research. Ask your critical friend to do the same. Look at your picture and ask, 'How do I position myself here? What assumptions do I bring to the process?' Talk it through with your critical friend, and see if they come up with similar ideas to yourself.

Do you see things in the same way or differently? Can you draw on each other's ideas to make sense of what you are doing in your different research programmes? How?

Can you share your ideas so that other people can use them? Perhaps you could communicate with others in your workplace, or create a website that enables other action researchers to develop similar ideas, and build up a gallery of visual representations.

REFLECTIVE QUESTIONS

Think about these questions.

✓ As an action researcher, can you think of ways to enable people (and yourself) to explain most effectively what you are doing? How?

✓ How can you draw on the ideas of others to help you develop your own?

✓ What other ways would be effective to show the differences between action research and traditional research, and how they can complement each other?

SUMMARY

This chapter has set out some of the main features of action research. It has outlined what action research is and what it is not. It has specifically said that action research is not necessarily the most appropriate methodology for all enquiries.

The chapter has encouraged you to come up with new ways to understand action research – for example, by using visualisation and creating mental models.

The chapter also makes the point that different methodologies can work together successfully.

We now turn to Part 2, which deals with issues about why you should do action research, and how doing action research can contribute to your own professional development.

PART 2

WHY SHOULD I DO ACTION RESEARCH?

This part enables you to see why you should do action research, and how it can help you in your work. It contains Chapters 7, 8, 9, 10 and 11.

Chapter 7 shows the relationship between action research and work-based learning, explaining that all action research is grounded in what may be understood as productive work.

Chapter 8 asks, 'How can action research help me as a practitioner?', and outlines how this may be possible.

Chapter 9 shows the relationship between action research and higher and continuing education: it is about accrediting work-based learning.

Chapter 10 asks, 'Where is action research located in research methodologies?', and explains where it has come from, what forces have shaped it, and how this has influenced the emergence of its present forms.

Chapter 11 asks, 'What if I am unemployed? Can action research help me then?', and goes on to discuss these issues.

Each chapter contains the idea that action research has always been associated with work-based learning. You can do action research to make sense of what you are doing, and to contribute to the new knowledge economy. You develop a new kind of professionalism that is grounded in the idea of collaborative working and democratic practices.

Chapter 7

Action research and work-based learning

This chapter is about how action research is linked with work-based learning. It contains the following ideas.

- Action research and work-based learning

- A brief history of action research

- Changes in the form of theory (for more advanced study)

ACTION RESEARCH AND WORK-BASED LEARNING

Action research has always been associated with work-based learning. This tradition began in the 1930s and has become more relevant in today's economic and political climates. It may even be a methodology for global economic recovery.

Practitioners across the professions and disciplines do action research. This means they evaluate their practices as they go, and also celebrate their professional on-the-job learning. Significant changes have happened in forms of professional education, as explained in the next chapter.

The most popular professions for action research remain education and nursing and health care (for example, Somekh 2006; Koch and Kralik 2006). However, action research has now branched into the general public services sectors, and is now entering business and industry, and even financial services and selling (Squire 2009).

To appreciate how this situation has come about, here is a brief history of action research. It will also help you locate where action research has come from and what any new focus may be.

A BRIEF HISTORY OF ACTION RESEARCH

Action research began in the USA in the 1930s, with the work of Kurt Lewin, a social scientist, and others. It actually began in other places as well, but Lewin's work is usually taken as the starting point. It was very popular for a time, especially among the teaching profession, through books such as Stephen Corey's (1953) *Action Research for Improving Practice*. However, the launch of Sputnik by Russia in 1957 and the political tensions that followed it in the USA led to a decline of interest in funding and support. Instead, a new focus on the need for excellence in what was to develop into a space race meant that money was diverted from education to state-of-the-art technologies.

CHANGES IN THE FORM OF THEORY

This next piece is more theoretical, but important if you are on a course, especially one for a degree.

The work of Jack Whitehead has been particularly influential in that he made a break with traditional views of theory. In Part I we said that the word 'theory' means, broadly speaking, 'explanation'. Traditionally, it was held that only higher education people could generate theories. The expectation was that practitioners would apply those theories to their practices, in order to improve what they were doing. Whitehead developed the idea in the 1970s and 1980s, radical at that time, that practitioners were capable of generating their own personal educational theories through the descriptions and explanations they offered for their practices. This view has been taken up today throughout the world. It is no longer seen as radical, and forms the basis for many professional education programmes.

However, this view carries implications because it means that practitioners have to explain how they hold themselves accountable for what they are doing, and this can be uncomfortable for some people. Doing action research as a form of professional education can be wonderfully enriching but it can also be risky.

Over the years, various models and different interpretations of action research have developed. Some people think it is important to get the technical steps and methods right. Other people are more interested in the values that underpin action research, such as a commitment to social justice and the idea that people should be in control of their own practices and the way that they conduct their work. These different perspectives make for healthy debate. While people are arguing, they think and question, and clarify their own ideas, which is a key strength of action researchers.

EXAMPLES OF DIFFERENT FORMS OF THEORY

Here are some examples of the use of different forms of theory.

Mara is a primary teacher. She enjoys the work of Piaget, and draws on his theories about the way that children's capacity for understanding develops. She applies his theories to her work with young children. She says, 'From Piaget's work, I can understand that children learn through their interactions in the world. They build up understandings that help them construct new ideas about how to deal with things, and about the nature of the things themselves.' Mara develops her teaching strategies according to these ideas. She uses traditional forms of theory to help her understand and make sense of her work. Traditional forms of theory, which tend to be abstract and conceptual, are often called 'propositional theories', because they make propositions about the objective world.

Fritz is also a primary teacher, and he also enjoys the work of Piaget. However, he prefers first to observe his own teaching, and find new ways of enabling children to develop deeper understandings of the relationship between themselves and the objects they construct. He says, 'I think I can show how children can build up understandings that help them to construct new ideas about how to deal with things, and the nature of things themselves, and I can also show and explain to you how I do this.' Fritz incorporates the ideas of Piaget into his own living theory of practice; he is able to explain what he is doing when he is teaching young children. He uses his own personal form of theory to help him understand and make sense of his work. In other words, he generates his own living theory, so called because it is embodied in the way he lives his life.

You can see many examples of practitioners' living theories on http://www.jeanmcniff.com and http://www.actionresearch.net. An increasing number of examples is available in books and web-based resources, covering a range of professions.

EXERCISE

Ask yourself the following:

How do you position yourself: as someone who applies other people's theories to your practice, or as someone who generates their own living theories from their practice, or a mixture of both?

In the answer you have just given, what choice did you make? Why did you make this one and not another?

Do you see any problematics in your position? What are they?

Can you think of any issues that others might see as problematic?

REFLECTIVE QUESTIONS

✓ Can you see the differences between traditional propositional theories and living theories?

✓ Can you see that these different forms are underpinned by different ways of thinking? (If you want to explore these ideas further, have a look at McNiff and Whitehead 2009, 2010 and 2011).

✓ Which forms of theory do you tend to use? The chances are that you use a mix. It is interesting – and important – to appreciate what kind you are using, and why you are using it.

SUMMARY

This chapter has explained how action research is located within the context of work-based learning. To consolidate the idea, the section has given a brief history of action research, and explained how different perceptions have led to different traditions, which in turn have led to the formation of different kinds of theory.

Now let's look at how action research can help you as a practitioner in your own workplace.

Chapter 8

How can action research help me as a practitioner?

This chapter is about how doing action research can help you as a practitioner in your own workplace. It contains advice about the following.

- Where can you do action research?
- Judging quality in work-based learning
- Self-evaluation for improving practices
- Professional assessment and appraisal

WHERE CAN YOU DO ACTION RESEARCH?

You can do action research virtually anywhere, but it is commonly recognised that there are two main contexts. The first is in workplaces, where practitioners study their work and try to improve it, sometimes within a wider focus on organisational development. If appropriate, they can have their work-based learning recognised, often in the form of in-house professional certificates, and also by using it as part of a higher degree programme of studies. This means that the second context is in higher education: this is dealt with in Chapter 9. Nowadays workplaces and higher education are strongly related. One of their main links is through finding ways to judge quality in workplace-based learning.

JUDGING QUALITY IN WORK-BASED LEARNING

An influential literature has emerged over recent years that shows why work-based learning should be seen as a valuable form of professional development, with potential for improved wellbeing for individuals and organisations through knowledge-creation (Schön 1983; Senge 1990; Nonaka and Takeuchi 1995). The potential value that on-the-job learning can bring to economic and societal growth is also recognised.

However, while the value of practice is appreciated, insufficient attention is paid to matters of ensuring quality in work-based learning. If people want their professional learning recognised, as they should, they also need to explain how they evaluate what they are doing, and identify any aspects that may need improvement. This means doing research into the practice, and explaining how and why the work should be judged good. This is where action research comes in, beginning with practitioners' self-evaluations.

SELF-EVALUATION FOR IMPROVING PRACTICES

The key question that action researchers ask is 'How do I improve my practice?' (Whitehead 1989). In many workplaces this question transforms into 'How do we improve our practices?' and some powerful accounts explain what is involved in transforming 'I' to 'we' (McNiff 2011). Practitioners take responsibility for evaluating and improving their own practices.

This perspective is quite different from a more traditional view of professional education. In traditional forms, the usual procedure is to bring in an acknowledged expert from an academic setting to offer advice or tell people what to do.

This situation is now seen as out of date, because practitioners themselves are understood as experts of their own practice, yet always willing to learn more and improve. You become your own expert adviser. This willingness to improve your practice is a sign of 21st century professionalism.

The question 'How do I improve my practice?' contains social and educational intent. The intent is that you improve your work for the benefit of others as well as yourself. If you can improve what you are doing, there is a good chance that you can influence the thinking of the other people you are working with. This could in turn influence systemic organisational transformation and improvement.

The methodology of action research also means that you have to carry out stringent validity checks on an ongoing basis (see Part 3). Are you really influencing people's thinking so that they can take control of their own ideas and actions? Or are you fooling yourself? How do you know?

PROFESSIONAL ASSESSMENT AND APPRAISAL

The shift from the outsider expert and knower to the insider expert and knower has led to a shift in the form of professional assessment. There is now a focus on incremental learning (formative evaluation), which recognises that people build on previous learning through developing their existing knowledge of practice. Practitioners can produce their professional portfolios to show the development of understanding of their learning and its potential influence for personal and social wellbeing.

Practitioners are therefore authorised to make judgements about the quality of their own work, while accepting the responsibility of making those personal judgements available to the critical scrutiny of their organisations and to general public scrutiny and evaluation. This is usually done through the production of reports, which is one of the reasons why practitioners need to know how to write good quality reports (Part 5).

EXAMPLE

Sue is an interior decorator. Her job is to advise clients on interior design and appearance. She attends a course at her local college to help her develop appropriate skills such as artwork, layout and use of colour. The lecturer points out what is involved in developing this expertise, and encourages her to experiment with her own ideas. Sue produces a portfolio of work for assessment. As part of her assessment, she is required to say why she has chosen specific designs, and what criteria she has used to make her selection. She negotiates her decisions about the quality of her work with her lecturer, prior to submitting the assignment.

EXERCISE

Think about these questions.

- Do you believe you can be your own expert? What do you need to do to get to this situation?
- Being your own expert means that you are able to make judgements about the quality of your work. How are you going to make these judgements? See Chapter 19.
- How do you think you can test the validity of those judgements? See further ideas in Chapters 18 and 19.
- Will you involve anyone else in helping you test the validity of your judgements? Who? Why will you involve these people and not others?

These kinds of questions are key to having your action research approved if you are on a formal professional development course, especially for higher education accreditation. Ideas about this are dealt with in the next chapter.

REFLECTIVE QUESTIONS

Ask yourself the following questions.

✓ Can I show that I have improved my work-based learning? How?

✓ How do I judge whether or not the practice has improved? What kind of criteria and standards do I use?

✓ Do I evaluate my practice regularly and systematically? How do I do this?

✓ Who do I get to check that any conclusions I arrive at are reasonably fair and accurate?

SUMMARY

This chapter has set out ideas about how you can improve your professionalism by undertaking your action enquiry. It has addressed issues of

• The settings in which action research can be done

• The links between action research and work-based learning

• The importance of self-evaluation for improving practices

• Changes in the nature of professional assessment and appraisal

---

This chapter has dealt with action research in the workplace. The next chapter deals with accrediting that action research, so we now move into higher education.

Chapter 9

Action Research and Higher and Continuing Education: Accrediting work-based learning

This chapter is about doing action research in higher and continuing education contexts, and getting it accredited. It contains two points.

- Accrediting work-based learning
- Action research and the new knowledge economy

ACCREDITING WORK-BASED LEARNING

If the first context for action research for professional learning is in workplaces, the second context is in higher education. Workplace-based practitioners can achieve their higher degrees through the production of their dissertations and theses that offer accounts of their work-based professional learning – see examples on http://wwww.jeanmcniff.com and http://www.actionresearch.net.

This situation has far-reaching implications for debates about who should be recognised as a knower, and about where knowledge and knowledge production is located. You need to know two things in this regard, as follows.

Work-based knowledge is now seen as completely valid

It is now generally recognised that the knowledge produced in workplaces is as valuable and valid as the kind of knowledge produced in universities, though the knowledge may take different forms. Also, nowadays many academic staff in universities see themselves as practitioners producing practice-based knowledge in a workplace, rather than as academics who produce only 'pure' knowledge. Gibbons et al (1994) speak about Mode 1 and Mode 2 types of knowledge. Mode 1 is traditional academic knowledge, the type usually communicated in traditional academic journals. Mode 2 is practice-based, or work-based knowledge. This kind of knowledge is also communicated in academic journals, though these journals would be more committed to celebrating reflective practice. These days both kinds of knowledge are seen as equally valid, which is good news for action researchers.

Academics do action research too

However, tensions still exist in many higher and continuing education contexts about which kind of knowledge informs different roles and responsibilities. Because many academic practitioners who work in universities and colleges also produce their accounts of professional learning while supporting the studies of workplace practitioners, universities tend to be seen now as workplaces where people work, though with special aims and purposes (Garnett et al 2009).

It has to be said, however, that many academics still see their role as handing out 'the knowledge' rather than as creating new knowledge in company with those whose studies they are officially supporting; but the situation is changing rapidly towards more democratic forms of working and a dialogue of equals. These tensions about roles and responsibilities will take time to resolve.

There is therefore currently a global focus on improving access for all practitioners to continuing and higher education for several reasons to do with sustainability, including the following.

ACTION RESEARCH AND THE NEW KNOWLEDGE ECONOMY

There is increased understanding, on a global scale, that doing action research can enable people to contribute to a new knowledge economy. Some of the main arguments are as follows.

- Many governments believe that more people should have access to a university education. This means that universities need to offer programmes that value different kinds of knowledge, ranging from 'academic' knowledge to practice-based knowledge.

- Many people in business and industry demand that university courses 'produce' graduates who have practical skills relevant to the production of new technologies and new forms of consumer goods.

- It is widely recognised that physical resources, such as oil and gas, will run out in a short time. It is therefore essential to move from a resources-based economy to a knowledge-based economy. More people need to learn how to develop the kind of skills and knowledge that will enable them to create new forms of resources and goods to sustain an ever-growing world population.

In recent years, the global economy has suffered severe setbacks, mainly through the non-regulated activities of a small group of financial and intellectual elites, who have control over wealth and knowledge. This crisis has revealed how important it is for work-based practitioners to show how they hold themselves accountable for what they do. It also reveals that practitioners need to up-skill themselves to ensure full employment for a healthy economy.

Action research is seen as a methodology that enables practitioners to meet all these demands. This is one of the reasons why it is important for you to do your action research and contribute to the debates from a position of informed knowledge. This theme is developed in Part 4.

EXAMPLE

Paulus is about to go to university to study entrepreneurialism. He has been involved in a workplace training scheme to help people learn how to learn. He has learned new thinking skills, including how to think laterally and critically, and how to tackle new tasks that have multiple solutions and to choose the most appropriate one. He has not studied a subject, such as English or Geography, but, using an action research approach, he has studied his practice across a range of contexts, such as practising for interviews and learning how to make presentations. These are the kinds of qualifications he needs to get onto this new course.

Paula has been a community worker for twenty years, and now wishes to return to formal study to get accreditation for her work. She finds that she can submit her professional learning for accreditation, by producing a professional portfolio that documents her experience, as well as her learning from that experience. She develops her portfolio using an action research framework (see Part 5), and submits it as part of her entry requirements for her higher education course.

EXERCISE

As part of your on-the-job learning, write out what you are doing that could contribute to the wellbeing and sustainability of your organisation. What are the potentials of your learning? How can you use it?

Now think about how your professional learning is helping you to contribute to wider debates about economic and societal renewal.

Do you read more? Do you think more actively? Do you interrogate what you read or hear on the news? Have you become more critical? Do you make your voice heard?

Thinking about issues like these can help you see the potential value in what you are already doing and what else you could do.

REFLECTIVE QUESTIONS

✓ Do you want to get your workplace-based learning recognised and accredited? Why?

✓ How do you intend to go about it?

✓ Are you confident about how to put together a professional portfolio? Look at Part 5 for some further ideas.

✓ Are you confident about your capacity to contribute to a new knowledge economy? You should be – you are a capable practitioner who is developing a research base for your practice. This is what is required to contribute to new ways of being in the world. An economy is not only about money: it is about people interacting with one another, using exchange mechanisms or currencies. Today's currency is still money, but tomorrow's currency will be knowledge. Your knowledge is as valuable as everyone else's. It is up to you to get your knowledge recognised and validated, and make your own special contribution in your own way.

SUMMARY

This chapter has addressed issues of how action research is located in higher and continuing education. It has focused specifically on new developments in accrediting action research for work-base learning in higher and continuing education contexts. It has made the point that attitudes by academic staff are changing significantly in relation to the knowledge base of their own roles and responsibilities. It has also made the point that new forms of economy will be knowledge based. This has implications for how you position yourself as a practitioner.

The next chapter is the most difficult one in the book, so look at it only if you wish to stretch your mind or if you are on a course leading to accreditation.

Chapter 10

Where is action research located in research methodologies?

This chapter is more theoretical than the rest of the book. It is important if you are on a degree course. If not, you can skip to Chapter 11.

The chapter makes the point that, if you wish to engage in higher education study, you need to understand where action research is located within research traditions, so that you can justify your choice of doing action research.

It deals with the following issues:

- Action research and the western intellectual tradition
- Research traditions
- Practitioners' living theories of practice
- Difficult questions

ACTION RESEARCH AND THE WESTERN INTELLECTUAL TRADITION

This chapter locates action research within other western intellectual traditions, as these have emerged and developed over time. Here you can read about the roots of action research, how it has developed, and where it may be going. Remember: in this book we are speaking about the western intellectual tradition; people in other parts of the world may see research differently.

Here is a brief history of different western research methodologies and how these influence forms of knowledge and theory.

RESEARCH TRADITIONS

As noted previously, research is about finding things out that were not known before: it is about generating new knowledge. People have done this throughout time, using different ways. In mediaeval times (roughly the millennium between the 5th and 16th centuries), people believed that you could explain what was happening and foretell the future by consulting the stars or reading runes. Even today, people believe that you can explain things by reading tealeaves or people's palms, and many people believe strongly in astrology. Others say this is superstition.

The period after mediaeval times became known as the Enlightenment. It marked the beginning of what is known today as scientific enquiry, which is based on rationality rather than superstition.

Empirical research

The first kind of rational research to emerge was empirical research. A researcher (in those days, researchers were also called philosophers) identified a particular situation, did experiments on it, and then observed what happened. The aim was to produce theories (descriptions and explanations) and tell stories about what was happening. What was studied at that time was the natural world such as rocks and trees.

The way the research was done (the methodology) was to manipulate variables to see whether a hypothesis could be demonstrated as tenable. This form of research remains strong today. For example, if you are the producer of Whizzo plant food, you test its effectiveness by using it on an experimental group of tomatoes, compared with a control group, to see whether the experimental group produces more, bigger, better tasting tomatoes. This is the basis of most scientific and technological enquiry.

Interpretive research

During the 1800s, new forms of qualitative research began to appear; that is, people began to shift from measuring things (quantitative analysis) to understanding their meanings (qualitative analysis). Researchers shifted their focus from rocks and trees, and began to study people. The aim was to generate new theories about how and why people behave as they do. This gave rise to disciplines such as sociology (theories about how people behave), psychology (theories about how people think) and philosophy (theories about what is good and truthful).

However, things began to get problematic, because, whereas rocks and trees do not answer back, people do. Researchers working in new research traditions such as anthropology and ethnography assumed that they could offer explanations (theories) for human behaviours. These 'grand theories' were indeed grand, but did not take individual differences into account – they simply made pronouncements about how 'people' are, as one standardised group. These descriptive theories then tended to become prescriptive, i.e. to say not only how people are but also how they should be; and the new disciplines of sociology and psychology began to make statements about how people should live and how their lives should be judged.

Critical research

From the 1920s and 1930s, a new tradition of critical theory began to emerge. Ideas developed about the need to engage critically with questions about how particular social situations come into being, and how political, economic, cultural and historical forces can shape people's lives. People started asking questions about taking action to change unsatisfactory aspects in order to improve their lives.

A distinctive feature of critical theory is, however, that, although researchers talked about the need to take action, they never actually took action themselves. Taking action needed a new form of action theory (see below).

Pause for thought – Whose theory? Whose practice?

The most important point to note throughout is that the person positioned as researcher still told the story. They still owned the theory because they got to offer the explanations, and to put the story into the public domain. In the case of critical theory, the external researcher continued to observe people as they talked about taking action. The external researcher produced theories (explanations) for why 'ordinary' people (practitioners) should take action and what kind of action they should take. Not surprisingly, this led to imbalances of power, where the 'expert knower' was more powerful than the 'trainee practitioner'.

However, this was all about to change ... read on.

Theories of action: action research

Many people began to see the need to turn the recommendations for action into real action; and new research traditions such as social activity theories and action research began to emerge that said (in principle) that people themselves could explain what they were doing when they took action. However, in spite of the rhetoric about equality and democratic dialogue, the reality was that traditional researchers still worked hard to maintain their power/knowledge, so the situation tended to stay the same: the 'expert' external observer continued to generate propositional theories about what people were doing and why they were doing it. It remained accepted that the researcher would generate the theory and the practitioner would apply it.

This situation remains for much traditional research today, and leads to what is known generally as the 'theory–practice gap': the theory remains with the external (academic) researcher, while the practitioners who are being studied apply the academic's theories to their practices. Theory and practice remain separate. Big ironies can be found in the literatures when academic researchers write stories about emancipatory forms of knowledge from their own positions as knowledge/power-holders.

However, new traditions are developing these days in that many academic practitioners are challenging traditional views, and new literatures show how academics themselves undertake their action enquiries to explain how they hold themselves accountable for their work (Tribal Education/McNiff 2010).

PRACTITIONERS' LIVING THEORIES OF PRACTICE

We saw earlier that a significant break happened in the 1970s, through the work of Jack Whitehead, who began to question the rationality and justice of traditional forms of theory. He wanted to develop a new form of theory that shifted the focus away from outsider to insider research. Insider researchers could now tell explanatory stories about their own practices. The stories were explanatory because they offered explanations for what the practitioner-researcher was doing, based on evidence from their research. This form of research has today become known variously as self-study, self-study action research, and autobiographical research. From this perspective, the aim of action researchers is always to generate their own living theories of practice as they engage with the question 'How do I improve what I am doing?' (Whitehead 1989).

This has been a real shift in paradigms, or sets of ideas and approaches (Kuhn 1964), and new research questions are being asked. Instead of asking, 'What are they doing? How can it be understood?', researchers now also ask, 'What am I doing? How do I understand it?'

DIFFICULT QUESTIONS

However, difficult questions remain, because the enduring questions are not only about doing research, but also about who has the power and how they use it. Those questions are generally:

- Whose practice? Whose research? Who researches whom? Does an external researcher research a practitioner's practice, or do they all research their own in collaboration with one another?

- Whose voice? Does an 'official' researcher speak on behalf of a practitioner, or does everyone speak for themselves?

- Whose theory? Does an official researcher offer explanations for what other people are doing, or do they all offer explanations for what they themselves are doing?

- Who speaks? Who is allowed to speak for themselves? What established practices are in place?

- Who says? Who makes decisions about these things?

This book takes the view that all practitioners are able to speak for themselves, and should do so, as far as they wish. It also takes the view, however, that if practitioners choose to speak for themselves, and wish to claim their work as quality work and their explanations as quality theories, they need to ensure that what they are doing is the best it can be. They also need to ensure that they communicate their ideas in ways that stand as high quality research and not just personal opinion. These ideas are developed in Part 3.

However, a key question arises for today's economic situation – What if you haven't got a job, or your business is struggling to survive? Can action research help then? These questions are the focus of Chapter 11.

EXERCISE

As a reminder to yourself, write answers to the following:

- Explain what a paradigm is, and what a paradigm shift is.

- Write out a brief summary of the main research traditions.

- Explain why self-study action research marks an important paradigm shift (think about the form of theory).

- Say what is important about practitioners' living theories of practice. Say what is important about your own.

REFLECTIVE QUESTIONS

Think about the following.

✓ Are you confident that you know the difference between different research traditions? Can you see how paradigms (sets of ideas and approaches) have shifted over time?

✓ Action research is part of a new paradigm that is grounded in the idea that knowledge must be located within a knower. Similarly, individuals can create their own theories, or explanations, for what they are doing. Do you see how you are part of this paradigm shift?

✓ How do you feel about being part of a revolution in ideas? Do you enjoy the idea, or is it too risky? Many people feel that they do not wish to move out of their comfortable situations, so they stick with the status quo. Other people prefer to be adventurous and try out new ideas. Where do you stand?

SUMMARY

This chapter has given a brief overview of where action research can be located within emerging methodological traditions. It traces the development of these traditions, and notes how action research initiated a change in the focus of theory, towards the living accounts of practitioners.

We now consider the difficult question: What if I am unemployed? Can action research help me then?

Chapter 11

What if I am unemployed? Can action research help me then?

This chapter asks the question, 'What if I am unemployed? What if my business is struggling? Can action research help me then?'

It contains the following points:

- Action research in context
- Undertaking your personal enquiry
- Building up a research-based professional portfolio
- Selling yourself

ACTION RESEARCH IN CONTEXT

We said in the previous section that any research methodology has to be understood within its current social, economic, political and cultural contexts. In 2010, therefore, action research has to be seen within a context of slow recovery from a deep economic recession, and it also needs to be seen as offering potential for ways out.

If you are caught up in the fall-out from the recession, the good news is that action research can help you create opportunities to get out of economic and personal difficulties, in a range of ways, including the following:

- Undertaking your personal enquiry
- Building up a research-based professional portfolio
- Selling yourself

There is of course no guarantee that you will get a job – the economic situation is still severe – but at least engaging in action research can help you develop new attitudes and new skills that should go some way to getting you going.

UNDERTAKING YOUR PERSONAL ENQUIRY

Doing action research means that you begin by taking stock of the present situation, identifying any aspects that need attention (in your case, that you haven't got a job), finding ways of improving it, and developing new ways of working. Your research question will therefore probably take the form, 'How do I get a job? How do I manage to keep my business going?'

Your answers would probably include taking stock of your current knowledge and skills, what you can offer, and how you can develop new ideas. Perhaps one of the most powerful aspects of action research is that you need to become inventive in your thinking, while recognising your own giftedness.

Ask yourself questions like these:

- What am I good at? Have I capacities and talents that I have not used in my previous employment that I could develop now?

- What do I know that others perhaps do not know? Do I have special talents and gifts that I can bring to new work contexts?

- What have I wanted to do all my life, yet never had the chance to do because I was too caught up in work? Should I take up a government training option, to help me develop my latent ambitions?

- What could I turn my hand to? What other jobs could I take up? Do I need to stay in the same place as I am now?

- How do I present myself to possible new employers? Do I need to practise interview skills?

- And so on …

The point is to consider all options, and try them out on a systematic basis. Do not reject any ideas that may help.

BUILDING UP A RESEARCH-BASED PROFESSIONAL PORTFOLIO

It can also be useful to record your activities in a professional portfolio. This is not simply a collection of activities you have undertaken, such as 'From 2000 to 2003 I was a veterinary assistant'. Instead, record aspects of your work and learning while you were doing this job: for example:

From 2000 to 2003 I was a veterinary assistant with Any Animals Veterinaries Ltd. During this time I had responsibility for the following:

- Ensure the wellbeing of animals that were brought in for treatment
- Negotiate the schedule of treatment with animal owners
- Work with others to communicate an atmosphere of competent professionalism

My professional learning was that

- I had to be prepared to work with others and understand their work-based needs
- I had to re-assess my own capabilities
- I found new, more effective ways of working with work colleagues and clients

By building up a professional portfolio like this, you are showing a possible future employer that you have developed an enquiring attitude to work, and that you are developing a research base for your own professionalism. You may still not get the job, but at least you are practising ways of digging yourself out of difficulties. You are also developing your self-esteem, and presenting yourself as a person who has much to offer and is not prepared to sit around waiting for other people to help them out. This is a key aspect of creating a demand for your services.

SELLING YOURSELF

If you are looking for a job, one of the most important things you can do is learn how to sell yourself. The time is right for new kinds of approaches to employment. People will probably not come knocking on your door: you have to learn how to knock on doors yourself, and offer a product (yourself) that people will want to buy.

Here are your main selling features:

- You have nurtured your own capacity for self-renewal through taking responsibility for your future.

- You explain how you understand what your strengths are and can bring them to new employment.

- You have experience and wisdom from previous learning-on-the-job and understand how you can use it.

- You have tenacity in continuing to improve your situation; you do not give up.

- You are positioning yourself as contributing to a new practice-based knowledge economy.

We have said throughout that a comprehensive shift is going on in the knowledge base of professional practices, in terms of what counts as knowledge and who is authorised to know. Everyone is seen as capable of knowledge creation, not just elites in universities. In fact, a certain role reversal is going on these days in that work-based learning now tends to be seen as a leading form of knowledge (Nonaka and Takeuchi 1995).

This view has tremendous implications for business and politics. It says that every person is capable of contributing to economic and social wellbeing through their capacity for knowing what they are doing. It also says that every person has the capacity to speak for themselves, and should do so, or be allowed to do so. This view has profound implications for the creation of a new public sphere (Part 4).

EXAMPLE

Reena is officially designated as having special learning needs, and she knows it. A year ago she was made redundant by the firm where she worked on an assembly line for computer parts. Recognising that she would have extra difficulties in finding a new job, Reena decided to avail of as many skills training programmes as possible, and learned how to do action research. This helped her to develop imaginative ways to cope with her situation; for example, she decided to save on her food bills by becoming self-sufficient. She used her small redundancy package to grow her own vegetables, which she also began to sell to friends and neighbours.

EXERCISE

Think about these questions, and write down the answers in your reflective journal. Do not look at what you have written for two days, then go back and think about it again.

- Have you been made redundant? What are you doing about it? Have you tried but still cannot get a job?

- Think of your special skills and attributes. What do you know that other people don't? What can you offer that other people can't?

- How can you sell yourself in your own special way? How do you develop your capacities even further?

- Write down six jobs that you do not think you could do. Now think of ways in which you could do them.

- Develop a professional portfolio using ideas from this book. Now go out and sell yourself.

REFLECTIVE QUESTIONS

Ask yourself these questions:

✓ Write down four things that other people can do that you can do too. Now write down two things that you can do that other people cannot do. Perhaps this is what makes you special. How can you build on it?

✓ What are your best features? How can you make the most of them?

✓ How do you explain to a potential employer that you have what it takes to get the job? Would a professional portfolio help?

✓ How do you cope in the face of multiple rejections? What kind of attitudes, skills and knowledge help to sustain you, so that you can try again?

✓ What is special about you? Look in the mirror. You see there a person of talent, a special person who deserves their place in this world. No one else can occupy your place; it is yours. Have faith in yourself, and go for it.

SUMMARY

This chapter has set out ideas to do with how undertaking your action enquiry can help you if you find yourself without a job, or in other difficult kinds of circumstances. It encourages you to build up a research-based professional portfolio so that prospective employers can see that you are not prepared to sit around but have learned how to make the most of your talents, and how to sell yourself, as well as raise your self-esteem and personal awareness of your value.

The question now arises, 'How do I do action research?' The next Part deals with this question.

PART 3

HOW DO I DO ACTION RESEARCH?

This part deals with the practicalities of doing action research. It contains Chapters 12, 13, 14, 15, 16, 17, 18, 19 and 20.

Chapter 12 asks, 'How do I do action research?' It sets out some key principles of doing action research.

Chapter 13 asks, 'How do I begin an action enquiry?', and gives advice about how to get started.

Chapter 14 outlines what is special about action research questions and how you can develop one.

Chapter 15 asks, 'Why am I concerned?', and explains that an appreciation of the links between values and practice can give a rationale for an action enquiry.

Chapter 16 asks, 'How do I show the situation as it is and as it develops?' It speaks about monitoring practice and gathering data.

Chapter 17 asks, 'What can I do? What will I do?' This chapter is all about taking action for specific purposes.

Chapter 18 asks, 'How do I show that any conclusions I come to are reasonably fair and accurate?' It sets out ideas about testing the validity of knowledge claims.

Chapter 19 asks, 'How do I explain the significance of my action research?' The importance of this aspect is prioritised here.

Chapter 20 asks, 'How do I modify my ideas and practices in light of my evaluation?' It gives ideas about possible new directions for your action enquiry.

Chapter 12
How do I do action research?

This chapter sets out the basic steps of an action enquiry. These take the form of critical questions that will help you make sense of what you are doing.

The chapter contains the following points.

- The basic principles of action research

- Developing your action plan

- Different models of action research cycles

- The idea of generative transformational evolutionary systems

- Some key points to remember about action research

THE BASIC PRINCIPLES OF ACTION RESEARCH

The basic steps of an action enquiry are these:

- I review my current practice,

- identify an area I wish to improve,

- imagine a way forward,

- try it out, monitor the action, and see if it works.

- I continue in this way if it does, or try another option if it doesn't;

- evaluate the new practice, and

- modify ideas and practices in light of the evaluation ...

(see also McNiff and Whitehead 2010)

Two processes are at work at the same time:

1 Your actions

You take action to try to improve the situation. For example,

- You try out a different seating arrangement for board meetings, so everyone will sit facing one another.
- You smile more when you greet customers.
- You add a new herb to your cooking.

2 Your learning

You learn through doing the actions. For example,

- You learn that people seem to communicate more effectively if they face one another.
- You find that smiling makes customers feel more comfortable (and generates more sales).
- You learn that some herbs add more flavour, so the food is tastier and people enjoy it more.

What you learn informs what you do, so it is important to gather data about your processes of learning as well as your actions on an ongoing basis. Always make sure you show the relationship between your learning and your actions when you write your report – always do this. Some researchers focus only on the actions and procedures, without talking about their learning, and this can weaken the authenticity of the research.

The action steps above show action reflection as a cycle of

- identify an area of practice to be investigated;
- imagine a solution;
- implement the solution;
- evaluate the solution;
- change practice in light of the evaluation …

(Whitehead 1989)

The action steps can now be turned into critical questions about how you are going to do your action research. This then forms your action plan.

DEVELOPING YOUR ACTION PLAN

Your action plan is as follows:

- What is my concern?

- Why am I concerned?

- How do I show the situation as it is and as it develops as I take action?

- What can I do? What will I do?

- How do I generate evidence from the data?

- How do I check that any conclusions I come to are reasonably fair and accurate?

- How do I explain the significance of my action research?

- How do I modify my ideas and practices in light of my evaluation?

(Whitehead 1989; McNiff and Whitehead 2006)

You can build your entire action enquiry around these questions.

DIFFERENT MODELS OF ACTION RESEARCH CYCLES

A number of models are available in the literature. Most of them regard practice as an action-reflection cycle, an approach that has been adapted in a number of texts, as follows:

- identify a problem
- imagine a solution
- implement the solution
- evaluate the solution
- modify practice
- identify a new problem …

… and you then work your way through a number of action reflection cycles …

NB This book does not see the beginning of an action-reflection cycle necessarily as a problem, so much as a situation that is somehow problematic, or intriguing, and that needs to be engaged with.

So one action research cycle can now turn into new action research cycles, as new areas of investigation emerge. It is possible to imagine a series of cycles to show the processes of developing practice. The processes can be shown as a spiral of cycles, where one issue forms the basis of another and, as one question is addressed, the answer to it generates new questions, as the example below shows.

Because of this cyclical action, the focus of your enquiry may shift, also as shown in the example.

The developing nature and possible shifting focus of your enquiry

You may experience something like the following.

Cycle 1

What is my concern?

I work in the toy manufacturing business, and I am concerned that business is falling off because of the global recession. I am also registered on a masters programme in business management, and I am using my enquiry as the basis for my dissertation.

Why am I concerned?

I am concerned because I want to maintain a high level of sales. Employees depend on me for their livelihoods; and I am dependent on my business too.

How do I show the situation as it is and as it develops as I take action?

I can show sales figures for the last two years and show a drop in profits.

What can I do? What will I do?

I can introduce new lines and try them out.

How do I generate evidence from the data?

I will see what the figures say at the end of the financial quarter. If they are healthy I will keep the new lines. If not, I will try other lines.

How do I check that any conclusions I come to are reasonably fair and accurate?

I will check my findings against the feedback of customers and employees.

How do I explain the significance of my action research?

I can explain how I am improving practice at the level of my work-based learning through adopting an entrepreneurial attitude. I can also show how I am improving my capacity to understand my work at a theoretical level.

How do I modify my ideas and practices in light of my evalua...

If things work, I will change direction in my business. I will als...
my new learning about framing my work as a systematic enquiry.

Cycle 2

What is my concern?

I have several concerns, and each of these could become a new action enquiry: for example,

- How do I find the best line in toys?
- How do I learn new marketing strategies for the new lines?
- How do I keep my business turning over well?
- How do I theorise my practice more adequately?

Remember that things do not often proceed in a neat, linear fashion. Most people experience action research as a zigzag process of continual review and re-adjustment. Research reports should communicate the seeming incoherence of the process in a coherent way. When you write your action research report, you should aim to write an account of at least one full action enquiry cycle.

THE IDEA OF GENERATIVE TRANSFORMATIONAL EVOLUTIONARY SYSTEMS

My own view is that we live in a deeply unified universe, where all things are connected, reminiscent of the 'butterfly effect', where the beat of a butterfly's wing can have repercussions in far-flung global terms. For me, all open-ended systems have the potential to transform themselves into more mature versions of themselves. Further, I see the whole of creation as coming into being, always in process, always growing. The visual representation I have developed to communicate these processes is an expanding spiral that cascades upwards (Figure 12.1). This visual can represent experiences, concepts, phenomena and practices. It is bounded only by one's mortality; and, in my philosophy, goes beyond death to engage in new forms of life.

Figure 12.1 *Representation of generative transformational evolutionary processes*

SOME KEY POINTS TO REMEMBER

Remember these distinctive things about action research:

- You are doing action research into your own practice, not other people's. You are the centre of your own enquiry: you speak in terms of 'I' (not 'the researcher' as in traditional research).

- You are trying out new, possibly better ways of working. You are not testing a hypothesis. The question that drives your research is 'How do I improve what I am doing?'

- Do not feel that you have to produce an answer or result (and do not let other people pressure you into thinking that you should). The best results take the form of new learning.

- You are working with other people, so you need to check your ideas with them and get their critical feedback on any conclusions you may be drawing.

- Try to keep your thinking open, and always hold it lightly. New ideas may emerge as you work your way through your enquiry. You are always allowed to change your mind. Changing your mind is the starting point for changing and improving your practice, which is what action research is all about.

EXERCISE

Try out these ideas:

- Draw a diagram, or some kind of graphic, to show how you see action research processes. Then draw a diagram, or graphic, to show how you intend to conduct your own action enquiry.

- Think of any other important questions you need to ask when planning and designing your action research. Check with your critical friend about how you could use them, and when.

- Go back to Chapter 3 and the example about learning how to ride a bike. See how the story in that example followed the action-reflection steps outlined here.

- Check that you appreciate action research as an integrated process. It is grounded in the question, 'How do I improve what I am doing?' and works systematically to a point where you can say with confidence, 'I have improved what I am doing.' This constitutes your claim to knowledge.

See other examples at http://www.actionresearch.net and http://www.jeanmcniff.com/reports.html

REFLECTIVE QUESTIONS

Ask yourself the following questions.

- ✓ Are you clear about the differences between traditional research and action research?

- ✓ Can you see that action research is open-ended and transformational?

- ✓ Can you think of an issue in your workplace that you need to investigate? How will you do this?

- ✓ How are you going to keep track of what you do and what you learn? What kind of data gathering methods are you going to use?

SUMMARY

This chapter has explained how to do action research. It has outlined basic principles and how to draw up an action plan. It explains that different models of action research exist in the literature; and you are invited to create your own. A key idea that informs the writing of this book is that of generative transformational evolutionary systems – this can be seen in the transformational form of action research itself.

The rest of this Part takes you through the steps and questions of an action enquiry. Chapter 13 deals with how you begin, by asking, 'How do I begin an action enquiry? What is my concern? What do I want to investigate?'

Chapter 13

How do I begin an action enquiry? What is my concern?

This chapter gives ideas about how you can begin your action enquiry. The chapter is about how you can find a focus, and contains the following points.

- Action planning
- What is my concern?
- Finding a research focus

Chapter 14 is about how you can formulate a research question.

ACTION PLANNING

We saw in the previous section that your action plan can look like this.

- What is my concern?
- Why am I concerned?
- How do I show the situation as it is and as it develops as I take action?
- What can I do? What will I do?
- How do I check that any conclusions I come to are reasonably fair and accurate?
- How do I explain the significance of my action research?
- How do I modify my ideas and practices in light of my evaluation?

WHAT IS MY CONCERN?

Your first question is, 'What is my concern?' This can also be phrased as, 'What am I interested in investigating?' or 'What do I need to find out more about?' Asking this question enables you to find a research focus.

You may regard this as a short-term project, when, as a student, you would ask a question such as, 'How do I make time to do my revision?' or a longer-term project, when, as a nurse, you would ask questions such as, 'How do I work with others to improve the quality of patient care?'

FINDING A RESEARCH FOCUS

A research focus can take different forms. Sometimes people focus on a *problem* issue, in which case they ask, 'How do I resolve this problem?' For example, they could ask, 'How do I encourage patients to take better care of themselves?' or 'How can I get a new job?'

Other people prefer to see the focus as a *problematic* issue, which means that they need to give the matter further thought and not simply take it simply at face value. For example, you may have a wonderfully functioning organisation, but what do you need to do to keep it so? You cannot just assume that things will always stay like this.

To help you identify a research issue, try this exercise.

Step 1
Think of your desk or your workspace. It probably looks busy.

Step 2
Think of the hundred things on the desk that all need urgent attention. Your day-to-day dilemma is often how you manage to attend to everything in the limited time you have.

Step 3
Now think of one issue that meets the following criteria:

- You *must* do something about it;
- You *can* do something about it;
- You *will* do something about it, starting tomorrow.

Step 4
Single that issue out from all the others on your desk and focus on it. What is going on with the issue that makes you want to investigate it further? Why are you prioritising that issue over others? Can you actually do something about it, and immediately?

Here are some examples of research issues:
- Sales are dropping in my area and I need to find ways of increasing them. This is a real issue for me because it is a matter of my livelihood.

- My students are not enthusiastic about their subject matters, and I am. This is a real issue because it is ruining the quality of my professional life.
- My patients get really nervous when they come for dental examinations. I would prefer them to be calm and have confidence in me as their dentist.

You have now found your research issue, or research focus.

Bear in mind that you need to keep your enquiry small, manageable and focused. Sometimes people choose topics that they cannot deal with: for example, they ask, 'How do I change the management structures of my organisation?' or 'How do I re-allocate the budget?' This kind of issue is way out of your control. However, what you can achieve is that if you begin investigating your own localised practice, and show that you can do things better, you have a greater chance of influencing organisational and workplace systems. You may even have a greater chance of influencing systemic practices of improvement.

Also bear in mind that you are focusing on your own practice, not someone else's. You cannot 'change' or 'improve' someone in a sustainable way. You can definitely change and improve other people in simplistic, short-term ways – for example, you can cut someone's hair or wash their face – but you cannot change them in such a way that they internalise the processes of change for themselves. Only they can do their learning for themselves; you cannot do it for them. The most you can hope to do is influence their learning so that they decide whether or not to improve themselves in ways that are right for them.

EXAMPLES

John is a tennis player, but his serve is not strong enough. He wants to improve his serve. He asks, 'How do I improve my serve?' He decides to find a tennis coach to help him.

Maria is a nurse. She needs to improve her technique of taking blood pressure. Learning how to take patients' blood pressure properly becomes her research issue. She decides to ask a senior nurse to help her find a better way.

Rafael is a teacher, but his students are not enthusiastic for his subject. His research focus becomes how he can encourage his students to enjoy his subject.

EXERCISE

Do the following:

- Think of a real issue that you need to do something about. This issue can be in your workplace, your home, or anywhere where you are active.

- Write down what the issue is.

- Tell your critical friend about it, and check with them whether they think you can do something about it. What if they say no? Will you give them more information, or something else? What do you need to do to persuade them to help you?

- Do you think you could do something about it, realistically?

REFLECTIVE QUESTIONS

Think about your research issue and ask yourself if it is feasible. Especially ask the following questions:

- ✓ Can I do something about it? Must I do something about it? Do I intend to do something about it?

- ✓ Ask also, 'Can I do this in the time I have, and with the resources I have?' If not, choose another issue.

- ✓ Check whether this research issue is feasible, if you are going to get the support of other people, and if you really can find ways to improve. If not, perhaps you should choose another topic.

If your answer is 'Yes' to all the questions, move to the next section.

SUMMARY

This chapter marks the beginning of your action enquiry. It has given advice about action planning, identifying a research issue that you must do something about, you can do something, and you will do something. These are priority criteria for a successful beginning to your action enquiry.

We now turn to the second part of beginning an action enquiry, which is to develop a research question.

Chapter 14
Developing a research question

This chapter is about developing a research question that arises from the concern you identified in Chapter 13. It contains the following ideas.

- How do I develop a research question?
- How research questions change
- Different starting points in action research and traditional research

HOW DO I DEVELOP A RESEARCH QUESTION?

Now that you have identified a research concern, the next step is to develop a research question.

You should aim to formulate a research question as soon as you can. At first your question may not be clear, and it may change. Most questions change as soon as the research begins. However, articulating it, even in a rough form, can give you a starting point.

Action research questions tend to take the form: 'How do I improve what I am doing?' (Whitehead 1989).

For example, you could ask,

- How do I find ways of increasing sales?
- How do I encourage my students to become enthusiastic for the subject?
- How do I inspire confidence in my patients?

Remember that your enquiry is about you studying your practice, so you need to accept the responsibility of asking the question. Do not expect other people to formulate questions for you.

Check that you are doing the following:

- You place your 'I' at the centre of enquiry.
- You ask how you can improve what you are doing.
- You are prepared to explain your learning processes to others.

- You are not put off by obstacles.
- You adopt an enquiring approach throughout.

HOW RESEARCH QUESTIONS CHANGE

People are sometimes surprised that their research question changes, but this tends to happen when you develop greater insights into the context. Also, your question often develops a new slant. For example, 'How do I inspire confidence in my customers?' can become, 'What am I doing now that does not inspire confidence? What do I need to do about my own practice?' The shifts in your research question can also lead to new action reflection cycles (see Chapter 12).

Remember also that any difficulties you are experiencing may be part of wider contexts. The question, 'How do I find ways of increasing sales?' may show that the particular area in which you are selling has dried up, so you now need to ask, 'How do I investigate new, more available lines of business?'

Formulating a research question is essential for your action research, because it gives you a firm starting point for your research journey. At the end of this part of your journey, when your reader (possibly examiner) reads your report, they will want to see whether you have engaged with the question. They will not expect you necessarily to 'answer' the question; most people appreciate that action research questions seldom get 'answered'. What usually happens is that the initial question tends to generate new, more interesting questions, which is part of the process of enquiry. What your reader really hopes to see is that you can engage with the problematics of trying to improve practice through research.

DIFFERENT STARTING POINTS IN ACTION RESEARCH AND TRADITIONAL RESEARCH

Also remember that the starting point in action research of asking a question is different from traditional research. In traditional research, it is usually a requirement to articulate aims and objectives for the research. These aims and objectives tend to be couched in behavioural terms, and as outcomes: for example, 'The person will be able to do x by the end of the enquiry'. Identifying and achieving behavioural aims and objectives is impossible in action research, because the whole point of the methodology is that you do not know where you are going until you get there, and new ideas and new scenarios emerge along the road as you get to different points. Also, where you arrive may not be where you planned to go in the first place, but you should be able to say that the new place is better than the place you started from, and that you are better informed about the processes involved.

It is however important to have a vision of where you wish to go, and you can articulate this in terms of your goals, or broad aims, as these are reflected in your values; but do not be persuaded to identify specific objectives, or behavioural outcomes. If there are any objectives in action research they are to encourage you to ask new questions and engage in new learning; and if there is any outcome it is improved learning to help you understand how you can improve your practice, and to influence others to do the same.

EXAMPLES

Here are some examples of how a research issue can generate a research question.

Issue: I need to find ways to encourage my students to study harder.

Question: How do I encourage my students to study harder?

Issue: I do not understand why productivity is falling off in my factory.

Question: How do I find out why productivity is falling off in my factory?

Issue: I need to get fitter. I am seriously out of shape.

Question: How do I get fitter and get back into shape?

EXERCISE

Go back to Chapter 13 and think about the research issue you identified there. Now formulate a research question for that issue.

Write down some more possible research issues that you would like to investigate and possible research questions.

Stay with your best question for a few days, and then reconsider it. Has it remained the same, or has it developed as you have thought about it? This often happens in action research, and you should not be unduly concerned about changing the question and the focus.

REFLECTIVE QUESTIONS

✓ Are you confident about the kind of questions you would ask in action research? Do not be pressured into asking questions about how you can test a hypothesis. Stay with asking about how you can improve something.

✓ Are you clear about the difference in starting points in action research and traditional research?

✓ Do you see how your initial research question is eventually going to turn into your knowledge claim? If you ask, 'How do I improve my practice?' your knowledge claim will be (hopefully), 'I have improved my practice.' You turn the research question into a research statement.

SUMMARY

This chapter has been about formulating a research question, of the form, 'How do I improve what I am doing?' It is a common experience that a research question will change during the research and a new one emerge. Bear in mind that traditional research and action research begin from different starting points, and therefore the form of their questions will be different.

You have identified your research issue and your research question, and you now need to offer reasons for doing and undertaking the research. This is discussed in the next chapter.

Chapter 15
Why am I concerned?

This chapter is about giving reasons for why you wish to do your action research, in terms of how you wish to live your values in your practice. It enables you to name your values. This will be important for later in your research.

The chapter addresses the following issues.

- Why am I concerned?
- An exercise in values
- A word of caution about values
- Experiencing oneself as a living contradiction

WHY AM I CONCERNED?

You are here in your action enquiry.

What is my concern?

Why am I concerned?

How do I show the situation as it is and as it develops as I take action?

What can I do? What will I do?

How do I check that any conclusions I come to are reasonably fair and accurate?

How do I explain the significance of my action research?

How do I modify my ideas and practices in light of my evaluation?

Asking the question, 'Why am I concerned?' is important because in all approaches it is important to give a rationale for the research, and say why it should be done in the first place. Unless you do this, your research could be seen as simply a good idea, but without a solid reason or purpose.

In traditional research the reason tends to be to establish a cause and effect relationship between variables – does applying Whizzo plant food result in a better yield of tomatoes?

In action research, the rationale tends to be to show how you are living your values in your practice. The issue of values and how you are living out your values is central in action research. For example, if you believe that all people have equal rights, you will try to organise your work so that everyone has the chance to exercise their rights.

AN EXERCISE IN VALUES

It can sometimes be difficult to articulate what our values are, so that we can live in line with them. To help you do this, try this exercise.

Step 1: What are your values? What do you believe in?

Think of why you do the work you do. Why are you a nurse, or a shopkeeper, or an army officer?

Write down for yourself, or tell a friend, or write an e-mail to them, explaining why you do what you do. Perhaps your reasons could be something like this:

- I came into nursing because I feel that I can help people live a healthy and fulfilling life.

- I became a shopkeeper because I believe that I can make a good living while also providing the community with what they need.

- I am an army officer because I believe that I need to contribute to the wellbeing of my country by protecting it.

Values are the things we value, the things that give meaning to our lives. The way we live shows how we try to make our values become real.

Step 2: Give a name to your values

Say what your values are, and give them a name. The people in the examples above could speak about the need for health and wellbeing, care, love, helpfulness, kindness, and so on.

Make a list of the values that inspire your life. Are they all equally important, or are some values more important than others? Do you prioritise certain values at different times?

Do you always live in the direction of your values?

Step 3: When was the last time you really lived your values?

Think of an episode in the last few weeks that really made your life worthwhile. Imagine that when you went home in the evening, you told your nearest and dearest about what happened. Perhaps you told them how you helped someone recover from a serious illness and one day that person sat up in bed for the first time in a month and asked for a hot meal.

Sometimes we focus only on the episodes where things did not go as we wanted them to, for whatever reason. Try to avoid doing this, and focus on what went well. By focusing on what went well, and explaining and demonstrating how you managed to influence the situation, you will position yourself as having greater capacity to influence things in the future.

What value-word can you put to what you have done? Perhaps you experienced 'a sense of well-being', or 'a desire to contribute to other people's happiness', or 'a sense of personal achievement'. Explain to a friend why these were important episodes for you, using the language of values. These values will become the standards by which you will eventually judge whether or not your practice has improved.

A WORD OF CAUTION ABOUT VALUES

Here is a word of caution about values.

The whole area of values can be tricky, because sometimes people speak about values as only those things that are socially acceptable, such as kindness or love or wellbeing. Some writers speak about 'personal and social good'; the 'good' stands as the realisation of values.

However, many people also hold values that others may not see as 'good' values. They hold ideas about 'the good' that others may not agree with. In her book *Eichmann in Jerusalem*, Hannah Arendt (1994) explains that Eichmann's view of a 'good society' was to maintain order by following rules, a view that contributed to the death of millions of Jews. Ideas about 'the good' always need to be problematised and located within their historical, social, political and economic contexts, and the understanding that one person's 'good' is not necessarily another's.

If you can articulate your values, and explain how you are trying to live them in your practice, you are well on the way to offering a justification for your action research. This will be part of your overall explanation for why you are doing it.

EXPERIENCING ONESELF AS A LIVING CONTRADICTION

However, let's return to the idea that sometimes, for a range of reasons, we do not live our values in our practices.

Whitehead (1989) says that we often experience ourselves as living contradictions when our values are denied in our practices. The issue then becomes what you can do about the situation so that you can overcome the contradiction and find ways of living in the direction of your values. This can act as a powerful place from which to begin your action enquiry.

In the example below, Katie tells her story of experiencing herself as a living contradiction.

EXAMPLE

My name is Katie and I am an administrator in an office. My job is to ensure that managers get to their meetings on time, and that the meeting rooms are ready. I enjoy my work, and I am proud of what I do. Last week everything seemed to go wrong, and nothing was ready for an important meeting. This completely went against everything I stand for, such as punctuality and professionalism. I got quite angry, and telephoned the facilities staff who should have organised the meeting room, and I must say I spoke quite sharply to them. Afterwards I felt guilty, because although it was their responsibility to ensure that things were properly prepared, it was my responsibility to work with them and make sure they felt supported in doing their job. I went to see them in their offices and apologised for my angry outburst.

EXERCISE

Think about these questions from the example.

- If Katie were doing her action research project, what kind of data could she gather to show the reality of experiencing herself as a living contradiction? What values would she wish to show in action?

- What could she do to put the situation right? How could she show her values in action?

- Think of your own present work situation. Are you living your values fully in your practice? If you are, can you produce data to show what your situation is like? (This point is developed further in Chapter 16.)

- Or are you perhaps not living your values as fully as you would like? If this is your experience, what can you do about it? (This point is developed further in Chapter 17.)

REFLECTIVE QUESTIONS

✓ Are you clear about why you need to give a rationale for your research?

✓ Are you completely comfortable with the idea that reasons for action are connected with values?

✓ Can you name your values? What are they? Can you explain why they are important?

✓ Do you always live out your values in practice? If not, why not? What do you need to do in order to live more in the direction of your values?

SUMMARY

This chapter asks the question, 'Why am I concerned?' Engaging with this question enables you to give a rationale and justification for your action research. Doing so involves identifying and articulating your values. It can also mean engaging with the problematic of recognising yourself as a living contradiction when your values are denied in your practice.

The question now becomes, if you are not living your values in your practice, what can you do about it? How do you resolve the tension of not living your values to the full? The next chapter has ideas about this.

Chapter 16
How do I show the situation as it is and as it develops?

This chapter deals with monitoring your practice, and gathering and analysing the data. These are important aspects that enable you to build an evidence base to ground your knowledge claims. The section contains the following ideas.

- Monitoring practice, and gathering and analysing data
- Frequently asked questions about gathering and analysing data
- Ethical issues

MONITORING PRACTICE AND GATHERING AND ANALYSING DATA

You are here in your action enquiry:

What is my concern?

Why am I concerned?

How do I show the situation as it is and as it develops as I take action?

What can I do? What will I do?

How do I check that any conclusions I come to are reasonably fair and accurate?

How do I explain the significance of my action research?

How do I modify my ideas and practices in light of my evaluation?

At this point you need to show your situation as it is. Are you living your values? Or not? How do you show the situation as it is so that other people can relate to what you are feeling? How can you show things as they are now, in this 'before' scenario?

You need to begin to monitor what you and other people are doing, and gather data. Your first set of data will act as baseline data, to show the situation as it is now. You will then continue to gather data to show the situation as it changes when you take action.

Throughout, bear in mind that action researchers, like all researchers, aim to make claims to knowledge. Because action research is about improving practice, your claim to knowledge should be that you have improved your practice, and also that you know how and why you have done so. Gathering data is a key piece of this because you will be able to show the developmental process from your original research question ('How do I improve my practice?') to your claim to knowledge ('I have improved my practice').

FREQUENTLY ASKED QUESTIONS ABOUT GATHERING AND ANALYSING DATA

Here are some frequently asked questions about gathering and analysing data.

When do I gather data?

Aim to gather data at the beginning of your project, so that people can see what the situation is like now, and why you are interested enough to get involved. You then gather data, or sets of data, on an ongoing basis, perhaps at regular intervals, but more likely when the opportunity arises.

What kind of data do I gather?

Your data shows the bridge between your initial research question – 'How do I encourage people to take part?' – and your knowledge claim – 'I have encouraged people to take part'. Always gather data with an eye to your research question, and keep to the point. You can compare later sets of data with earlier ones so that you can see progress. The data you gather is therefore always in relation to your research question, and how this transforms into your knowledge claim. It may help to imagine a tennis or a cricket match, where one player bats the question to the other, 'How do I improve my practice?' and the other bats it back in the form of a claim, 'I know how I have improved my practice'.

What happens if my data show me what I don't want to see?

This is called disconfirming data, when events show you what you do not want to see, for example, people are not as cooperative as you wish. This is important data and should not be swept under a carpet. If things are not going as you want, it is up to you to change what you are doing. You should also explain in your research report that you have done this, and why. Examiners love to see it when researchers reflect critically on their practice and research and take appropriate action. Action research is not about getting things right so much as learning how to do things better. Examiners want to see your learning as much as they want to see your actions.

How do I gather data?

Many different data gathering methods are available to you, both quantitative and qualitative. You can use surveys and attitude scales, head-counts, pre- and post-tests, and also journals, diaries, field notes, and audio and videotape recordings. Multimedia are especially powerful for showing the live experiences of people in the moment. Social networking such as e-mails, blogs, chat-rooms and websites also provide important data.

Do I gather data about myself only or about other people too?

Remember you are not studying other people. You are studying yourself, in relation with other people, and how you are influencing your own and their learning, in order to influence your individual and collective actions. Your data should therefore show what is happening in the following fields:

- Your learning, and how this is influencing your actions
- How your learning and actions are influencing other people's learning and actions (see Figure 16.1 below)

My learning	Other people's learning
My actions	Other people's actions

Figure 16.1 *Aspects you can gather data about*

Ultimately you are hoping to show how you have improved your learning in order to improve your actions; and you then want to show how you are influencing other people's learning so that they also improve their own actions. All these issues are interrelated and mutually influential.

What do I do with my data?

Aim to develop a data archive where you can store your data. This can be a box in your office or living room, or a folder on your computer. As you go, sort your data into categories such as 'conversations' or 'letters'. Keep your archive live, and re-arrange categories as necessary. You will need everything to be in order when it comes to generating evidence from your data.

ETHICAL CONSIDERATIONS

Ethical considerations are a major aspect of doing good quality research. Ethics refers to good attitudes and behaviours towards others in relation to yourself, and good attitudes and behaviours towards yourself in relation to others. The main principle is to do no harm.

Within all these multifaceted relationships, key aspects that you must attend to are as follows:

- Always ask and obtain people's permission to do research with them. Distribute ethics statements to all participants, as well as written letters asking permission to gather data. Keep copies of signed returns in your data archive.

- Promise confidentiality unless participants specifically ask for information about themselves to be made public.

- Assure participants that they may see all data about themselves whenever they wish, and that the data will be destroyed at the end of the project wherever possible.

- Confirm that they have the right to withdraw at any time, and that all data about them will be destroyed if they do.

- Maintain honourable conduct throughout.

EXAMPLE

My name is Carla and I am a chiropodist. In my profession, we must undertake regular professional development, and produce our professional portfolios to show our learning on the job. I therefore regularly evaluate my practice, which means that I have to gather feedback from clients about their level of satisfaction with my work. I gather data in the form of questionnaires and surveys, as well as personal interviews. The data I gather focuses on the level of client satisfaction. I use the feedback to inform my future practices. For example, I have learned that some clients prefer to sit up rather than lie down when I am attending to their feet, so I adjust my consulting room and my own seating arrangement to accommodate their wishes. I never speak about one client to another, and I maintain confidential records at all times in my password-protected computer, and as hard copy in a locked filing cabinet.

EXERCISE

Try this exercise to help you get a sense of how to gather data.

Draw a picture of your situation as it is at the moment. You do not need to produce an elegant drawing. You can use stick figures or symbols or any kind of graphic that suits. Now show that picture to a partner and explain to them what is happening in your situation.

Now imagine that you have started to take action, and move forward in time, say two or three weeks, or a month. Draw a second picture to show the new situation, and explain to a partner what you have done in order to move things on. Also explain to them how you have monitored the situation so that you can show the systematic nature of your enquiry.

You can use this exercise in any kind of professional education context. It is invariably enjoyable and enables people to see how they need to gather data systematically over time to show the developing situation. Just keep in mind, however, that when you come to put it into practice, things may not turn out as neatly as you expect.

REFLECTIVE QUESTIONS

Here are some more questions to think about.

Question: What kind of data gathering technique should I use at any one time?

Answer: You should use the technique most appropriate to enable you to gather data in relation to your research question. If your question is, 'How do I make staff meetings more interesting?' you will need to use a technique to capture the initial situation in which staff meetings are not especially interesting. You could use:

- Videotape, to capture the live action of staff meetings
- Surveys, to get people's opinions of staff meetings
- Field notes, to record your impressions of staff meetings
- Focus group interviews, to get ideas from key people of what they think of staff meetings
- Social networking processes such as Facebook.

Question: Should I monitor every piece of action?

Answer: It is virtually impossible to monitor and record every piece of action. Decide which action you are going to look for, in relation to your research question, and try to keep systematic records of that. The key is your research question, because your question is going to turn into your claim to knowledge. The data you are gathering will turn into evidence that will ground your claim to knowledge (see Chapter 18).

Question: What do I do with my data as I gather it?

Answer: Keep your data carefully and aim to build up a data archive. Try to sort your data into categories as you go (conversations; letters; tape recordings), and re-shuffle the categories as appropriate (responses from participants; records of your own learning; observers' comments). Do not throw data out too soon; your thinking will change over time, and the data you thought was irrelevant may turn out to be absolutely key.

Now, thinking about yourself ...

✓ Are you confident that you can use different kinds of data gathering methods at different times during your research?

✓ Can you see the relationship between your learning and actions, and the learning and actions of your participants?

✓ Are you confident about the idea of ethical issues, and the need to pay attention to detail?

✓ Are you clear about why you should gather data?

SUMMARY

This chapter has dealt with issues of monitoring practice and gathering and analysing data. It has engaged with some frequently asked questions about the field. It has also emphasised the importance of ethical considerations.

So, having established how you are going to monitor your practice and gather data over time, you now need to think about what action you are going to take in order to try to improve the situation. This is dealt with in the next chapter.

Chapter 17

What can I do about it? What will I do?

This chapter is about taking action, as you ask critical questions. It contains ideas about the following.

- What can I do about the situation? What will I do?
- Taking action
- What kind of action?
- What do I do now?

WHAT CAN I DO ABOUT THE SITUATION? WHAT WILL I DO?

You are here in your action enquiry:

What is my concern?

Why am I concerned?

How do I show the situation as it is and as it develops as I take action?

What can I do? What will I do?

How do I check that any conclusions I come to are reasonably fair and accurate?

How do I explain the significance of my action research?

How do I modify my ideas and practices in light of my evaluation?

You have gathered baseline data to show the situation as it is at the beginning of your project, in a state where you have to take action. You therefore need to think about what you are going to do now.

TAKING ACTION

Taking action is not an ad hoc affair. Your actions should be as planned and strategic as possible.

You might at this stage consult with other people, such as your critical friends, about ways in which you can move things forward. However, any decisions about action need to be your own. You are investigating your own work and your professional situation, and you are improving your learning all the time, so you need to retain ownership of any actions you take. You need to consider your options carefully and decide what you can expect to achieve, given the time, energy and other resources you have.

Bear in mind that things may not go as planned, and do not be disheartened if things fall apart. You are working with real people within real social systems, and people do not always act as you wish. It is your responsibility to walk with people, not expect them to walk with you.

Also bear in mind that your own thinking is bound to change. You may decide that you should not have acted in a particular way, so you will need to go back and change something. Action research is full of twists and turns, and things are seldom predictable.

WHAT KIND OF ACTION?

Consider also the kinds of actions available to you. You can take many kinds of action. You can take

- *forceful action*, where you tell other people what to do;
- *democratic action,* where you negotiate with others what you should all do;
- *subversive action*, where you question the status quo and try to change it;
- *educational action,* where you try to encourage people to think and act for themselves
- ... and so on.

Because action research is about trying to improve learning and thinking in order to improve social action, the most appropriate form of action is educational action. This is also how your practice can turn into praxis – morally committed action, with best personal and social intent in mind.

WHAT DO I DO NOW?

Having decided on a possible course of action, you now need to try it out. It may work and it may not. If it does, you will probably want to continue developing it. If it doesn't, you may well decide to abandon it and try something else. Just make sure you keep a record of what you do, so that your reader can see how your decisions were not willy-nilly but grounded in careful and wise thinking, often in negotiation with others.

... and keep monitoring the action and gathering data

You need to continue monitoring things and gathering data to see whether you are influencing the learning – of other people and yourself – and whether the learning is leading to new actions. You need to keep gathering the data to show a difference from the initial situation, and how things have developed as you move through your enquiry. Hopefully things are moving in the direction of what you believe in; perhaps people are beginning to participate more, or act more democratically, as you hoped they would.

The way in which you gather new sets of data can be the same, or different, from the way in which you gathered your first. You can use a survey method for both sets, and the difference may be highlighted in the responses that people give. Or you may audiotape your first set, and analyse your transcripts, and then videotape the next, and analyse those. You should decide whatever is right for you. You may be as creative as you wish or need to be.

EXAMPLE

My name is Ken and I am an automobile mechanic in a small garage. I am registered for a course leading to a certificate of engineering with our local college. A requirement is to do an action research project. I chose to study my practice as I carried out services on cars. My idea was that a car service could be done twice as quickly and efficiently if two mechanics worked together systematically through a car that was in for service. I teamed up with my friend Sam, and we timed ourselves as we worked separately on cars and then together. We kept records of our times and compared them as we worked on different cars. Judging from our results, our teamwork seemed to be more effective than working separately. We definitely seemed to make greater progress. There are added benefits also in that we learn from each other, and we learn to do things differently. We also had good fun. I will write this up for my project under the 'What can I do?' section.

EXERCISE

Think about the following:

Is it always possible to take action? Sometimes organisational constraints are too large: for example, you cannot take action to change the management system of your organisation. Be realistic. Keep your project small, focused and manageable. Do what you can with the resources you have, and do not try to do anything beyond your means.

Make sure you keep track of what you are doing and learning all the time, and also what other people are doing. You need to work out your own system of gathering data and storing it for later analysis.

Remember to link your actions with your reasons for action. If you feel that you need to inspire people to do better, you will act in an energetic way, from your values of high energy commitment; whereas if you feel that you need to listen more carefully, you will act in accordance with your values of respectful silence and compassion.

REFLECTIVE QUESTIONS

Think about these questions.

✓ Have you some good ideas about what you can do about your situation? If so, what will you do?

✓ What kind of action do you intend to take? Why this kind of action and not another?

✓ What do you think will happen? Have you thought about the consequences of what you intend to do?

✓ How will you continue to monitor the action and your learning?

SUMMARY

This chapter has engaged with ideas about taking action in the hope of improving your existing situation, and by trying to realise your values in your practice. It has discussed some different kinds of action available to you, and how you can monitor the action you decide to take, and gather and analyse data about what happens.

Having taken action and gathered and analysed data about what you are doing, you now need to generate evidence, in which to ground your claims to knowledge. Advice about this appears in Chapter 18.

How do I generate evidence from the data?

This chapter deals with issues of generating evidence from the data. This is one of the most important issues in doing research, because it is about demonstrating the truthfulness of your claims that you have improved practice.

The chapter contains ideas about the following.

- How do I generate evidence from the data?
- Why is this issue important?
- Identifying criteria
- Generating evidence from the data
- Showing the authenticity of the evidence

HOW DO I GENERATE EVIDENCE FROM THE DATA?

You are here in your action enquiry:

What is my concern?

Why am I concerned?

How do I show the situation as it is and as it develops as I take action?

What can I do? What will I do?

How do I generate evidence from the data?

How do I check that any conclusions I come to are reasonably fair and accurate?

How do I explain the significance of my action research?

How do I modify my ideas and practices in light of my evaluation?

WHY IS THIS ISSUE IMPORTANT?

Appreciating the importance of generating evidence from data is key in action research, for the following reasons. If you say, 'I have improved my practice', you can expect someone to say, 'Prove it.' Your answer here is that you cannot prove anything, but you can produce reasonable evidence to show that what you are saying happened really did happen and you are not making things up. You are saying that you are telling the truth, and people should believe you. In research language, you are saying that your knowledge claim is valid.

However, you do not expect people to take your assertion that your knowledge claim is valid at face value. You set out to test this validity. Through satisfying themselves that they can believe you, people then have greater confidence in your judgements about the quality of your practice and research, and you can too.

The way to test the validity of knowledge claims involves the following:

- Identifying criteria
- Generating evidence from the data
- Showing the authenticity of the evidence

IDENTIFYING CRITERIA

When you make judgements about things, including the validity of knowledge claims, you use specific criteria. For example, the criteria for choosing a coat could include fit and price and whether it keeps you warm. You would choose one coat rather than another in terms of which fitted you best, which was more affordable, and which keeps you warmest. You select the criteria in terms of your identified needs and your context.

In action research, your criteria take the form of your values. You judge the quality of your practice and research in relation to whether or not you can show that you are realising your values in action. For example, you judge the quality of your dental practice in terms of whether people feel nervous or at ease when they come in for a check-up. You judge the quality of your gardening in terms of how many flowers bloom and for how long. Your values of human and environmental wellbeing show through in both cases.

This is why it is so important to articulate your values at the beginning of your action research project. Your values emerge through your practice in a range of ways: as criteria, conceptual frameworks, and standards of judgement.

GENERATING EVIDENCE FROM THE DATA

Imagine you go shopping for a special gift for a friend. You go into a large shopping store with thousands of goods. Obviously not all are suitable for your friend, but perhaps twenty are. You have to narrow down your options to those twenty.

However, because you cannot afford all twenty, you have to choose, so you ask yourself, 'Which one is best for my friend?' Perhaps you make your choice based on cost, appropriateness, appeal, availability, and so on. These are your criteria. Guided by your criteria, you choose one item as your gift to your friend.

It is the same process when looking at your data. Your job at this point in your research is to think about how you can demonstrate the validity of your knowledge claim, so you search your data archive, using specific criteria, to find the right pieces of data for the job. These will be the pieces that you consider best demonstrate your claim in action. So if your research claim is 'I have encouraged people to be cooperative', you will look for those pieces of data that show people being cooperative. Your value of cooperation becomes real. Your value of cooperation stands as your real-life criterion. (But remember that you may be confronted with disconfirming data: you may experience episodes when people are not cooperative, which means you may need to re-think what you are doing.) You now drag those pieces of data out of one place – your data archive – and drop them into another place – your evidence archive. The pieces of data now transform into evidence, i.e. the special pieces of data that demonstrate your values in action. In research language, you achieve your nominated criteria, as these embody your values.

SHOWING THE AUTHENTICITY OF THE EVIDENCE

Even at this stage, however, the issue of truthfulness does not go away. Who is to say you have not made up your data? How do you show the authenticity of your data, so that your evidence base can be seen as honest and true?

The answer is that you should try to authenticate your data as you collect it, wherever possible, usually by making your sources evident. When you take a photo, make sure that the date and time appear on the photo. When you refer to an e-mail, place the original e-mail in your report, or in an archive, so that people can see the date, time, and source. If you refer to your field notes, make sure you place the date on the field note. If you refer to some correspondence, ask the sender to sign and date it. Do whatever you can to show the authenticity of your data.

When you report back to people, such as in a validation group or examination board, have your evidence base to hand as much as possible. For many people, this will take the form of material on your computer. Take a sensible approach and always ask yourself, 'What will it take for people to believe me?'

EXAMPLE

My name is Elsa and I am on a foundation degree course in fine arts. For my work placement, I work in a florists shop to learn how to do flower design. I think I am finally making progress in this regard. When I first came here three weeks ago I was useless at arranging flowers. I cut the stems too short and put the wrong flowers at the back and front of the design. My supervisor encouraged me to take photos of my creations at regular intervals, and Sue, the girl who owns the shop, also encouraged me to stick with it and not give up. I did what she advised, and read books on flower arranging, and learned to go with my instinct about which flowers were best suited to different arrangements. My photos showed distinct improvement over time – and I now also use up fewer flowers! I am getting quite proficient at flower arranging, though I still have a long way to go. I can show you photos of beautiful designs that entirely fulfil the criteria of aesthetic sensitivity required by the university. These are the photos I will take out of my data archive and submit as evidence of my developing expertise in my professional portfolio. I think I may make it after all.

EXERCISE

Do the following exercise in your reflective journal.

- Write down your research question. Respond to the question, 'What is my concern?'

- Write down your values. Say whether you are living your values in your practice. If you are, can you show it? If not, is the situation turning into a problem? Respond to the question, 'Why am I concerned?'

- Produce data to show the situation as it is. Say whether this represents the living out or the denial of your values.

- Say what actions you have taken to address the situation. Have you been successful? If so, say so. If not, say why not.

- Search your data to find pieces that will stand as evidence to back up any claims you make – whether these claims are that you are succeeding in influencing the situation for the better, or if things are not going according to plan. Drag these pieces of data out of the data archive and drop them into a new evidence base.

- Match the pieces of evidence with the claims. If you say, 'People are cooperating these days', produce evidence to show the realities of people cooperating. If you say, 'I need to try a different strategy', produce evidence to show why this may be the case.

Important note

Many books on action research do not make any distinction between data and evidence, and they do not explain that it is necessary to show how you make judgements about the quality of your action research. It is however essential that you know the differences, and can explain why it is important to know them. This is especially so if you are on an accredited course, where your examiners will want to see that you understand these things.

REFLECTIVE QUESTIONS

Ask yourself these questions:

- ✓ Are you clear about the difference between data and evidence?
- ✓ Can you see the importance of being clear about the difference?
- ✓ Can you explain why it is important to identify criteria for making judgements about quality?
- ✓ Can you explain how values transform into criteria and standards of judgement?
- ✓ Why is it important to pay attention to disconfirming data?

SUMMARY

This section has set out ideas about the processes involved in generating evidence from the data. These processes involve identifying criteria against which you can test the authenticity of the data and evidence within the broader exercise of testing the validity (or truthfulness) of the claim itself. It is important that you become confident around these processes, because paying attention to these issues of methodological rigour will establish the high quality of your action research in public perceptions.

Now that you have generated your evidence, you need to present it, together with your knowledge claim, to the critical scrutiny of others, to see if they agree with you. How you do this is told in the next chapter.

Chapter 19

How do I check that any conclusions I come to are reasonably fair and accurate?

This chapter continues the theme of testing the validity of your knowledge claims. We now move from grounding the claim in your evidence base, towards testing the validity of the claim, and the authenticity of your evidence base, against other people's critical feedback.

The chapter contains ideas about the following points.

- How do I show that any conclusions I come to are reasonably fair and accurate?

- What is important about this issue?
- Which people will you talk with?
- How do they make judgements about what you are claiming?
- When can you make your knowledge public?

HOW DO I CHECK THAT ANY CONCLUSIONS I COME TO ARE REASONABLY FAIR AND ACCURATE?

You are here in your action enquiry:

What is my concern?

Why am I concerned?

How do I show the situation as it is and as it develops as I take action?

What can I do? What will I do?

How do I generate evidence from the data?

How do I check that any conclusions I come to are reasonably fair and accurate?

How do I explain the significance of my research?

How do I modify my ideas and practices in light of my evaluation?

WHAT IS IMPORTANT ABOUT THIS ISSUE?

In the last chapter we talked about the importance of providing authenticated evidence to show the validity of your knowledge claims. However, this is still not enough to satisfy sceptics or to demonstrate methodological rigour.

You now need to show your findings to other people, and invite their critical feedback. This will enable you to say that you have tested your claims to the best of your ability, and it is not now only a matter of your opinion.

WHICH PEOPLE WILL YOU TALK WITH?

Here are the people you should talk with.

Critical friends

You have talked with critical friends throughout your research. You need them now to look at your criteria, and your data and evidence, and agree with you (or not) whether you are demonstrating good research practice. If they say that you need to do things differently, listen carefully and then choose whether or not to act on their advice.

Your validation group

You should set up a validation group to listen to your research reports at strategic intervals. Your validation group always acts as a group, whereas you can meet critical friends individually or in pairs or small groups. The validation group may be between four and ten people and should comprise people whose opinions you value. You should listen to their feedback and act on it. They may point out to you that you have to go back and do things differently, or provide further and perhaps more robust evidence.

HOW DO THEY MAKE JUDGEMENTS ABOUT WHAT YOU ARE CLAIMING?

The job of critical friends and validation groups is to provide critical feedback on your reports, and specifically about the validity of your knowledge claims. They would do this, acting from specific criteria.

They would ask themselves the following questions:

- Are you speaking in a way that they can understand you?

- Are you demonstrating your integrity by producing authenticated evidence to back up your knowledge claims?

- Do you demonstrate your authenticity by acting, over time, in a way that people can see how you are trying to live in the direction of your values?

- Do you show that you are aware that you are not doing your action research in a vacuum; that you are aware of contextualising factors, such as the local environment, or political issues, or ongoing dynamics in relationships?

- Do you demonstrate your capacity to reflect critically on what you are saying? Do you show your understanding that you could have done things differently?

- Do you make clear your understanding of the significance and implications of your action research?

WHEN CAN YOU MAKE YOUR KNOWLEDGE CLAIM PUBLIC?

You can make your knowledge claim public now. Once you have received the critical feedback of your validation groups, you can go ahead and make your claim to knowledge with confidence.

Be aware, however, that things will continue to change; this includes your knowledge claim. You should always hold your knowledge lightly, and be aware that what you know today may change tomorrow. Always remember that you may, after all, be mistaken.

EXAMPLE

My name is Matteus and I am a middle manager in a factory that bottles water. We pride ourselves on the purity of our water, and take this as the distinctive feature in our marketing and advertising. My task is to ensure ongoing quality control of our water. I have undertaken my action enquiry into my practice, as part of my work-based learning, and I have taken the issue of ensuring quality as the focus of my research. One aspect of the research was to investigate the shape and colour of the bottle we would put the water into. I gathered data on a systematic basis about public preferences as to the best shape and colour of bottle. I have a comprehensive data archive that indicates that people prefer long elegant bottles of pale blue. They also tend to prefer glass rather than plastic. I have generated strong evidence from the data about these preferences, and have presented my recommendations to the board of managers. I am now going to meet with them, to hear their verdict on my recommendations. I hope they agree that my conclusions are reasonably fair and accurate, and will agree to the production of long pale blue glass bottles. If so, perhaps I can look forward to a nice bonus.

EXERCISE

Think about the procedures for testing and demonstrating the validity of claims to knowledge as a game with specific rules. Here is how to play it.

Playing the validity game

First, write out your knowledge claim. Here are some examples:

- I am claiming that I have encouraged people in my organisation to work more co-operatively.

- I am organising my workload more efficiently these days and my productivity has increased.

- The patients in my waiting room are more at ease.

Second, talk through the steps involved in demonstrating the validity of these claims with another researcher. Give each other a mark for the validity of each statement; you may also award half marks as appropriate.

1. I identified a research issue.
2. I formulated a research question.
3. I articulated my values to say why I chose the issue.
4. I gathered data to show the situation in its initial state.
5. I consulted periodically with critical friends.
6. I took action to try to improve what I was doing in the situation.
7. I continued to gather data to show the situation as it evolved.
8. I sorted, categorised, analysed and interpreted the data on an ongoing basis.
9. I identified criteria for selecting evidence.
10. I generated evidence from the data.
11. I tested the robustness of the evidence against the critical feedback of my critical friends.
12. I convened a validation group and presented my provisional research findings; I invited their feedback in relation to articulated criteria and standards.
13. I am making my claim to knowledge with confidence.

REFLECTIVE QUESTIONS

Ask yourself the following questions.

✓ Are you clear about which knowledge claim you are making? What is it? Can you write it down?

✓ Are you sure you have sufficient evidence in which to ground your claim?

✓ Is your evidence authenticated?

✓ Have you tested the validity of the claim against the feedback of your critical friends?

✓ Are you sufficiently confident in the validity of your claim to present it in public, perhaps to a validation group or similar? Can you argue your case and defend your stance?

SUMMARY

This chapter has dealt with issues of testing the validity of evidence and of knowledge claims. It is a key area for establishing the credibility of your research, and of yourself as a researcher. It involves checking with people such as your critical friends and validation groups to show that you are aware of the need for public authentication of what you feel may be the case – just to check that you are still holding your knowledge lightly until it has been publicly approved as valid and legitimate.

A key aspect of presenting your knowledge claim for public validation is the capacity to articulate its significance, or importance. This brings in the idea of legitimacy. We turn to these issues in the next chapter.

Chapter 20
How do I explain the significance of my action research?

A main aspect of presenting your action research for public approval is your capacity to explain why your research is important, and why people should take you seriously and listen to what you have to say. This means you have to articulate the significance of what you have been doing. This chapter helps you to do this. It contains ideas about the following issues.

- How do you explain the significance of your action research?

- What is the significance, or importance, of your action research?

- Why is it important that you should explain the significance of your action research?

- How articulating the significance of your action research can give it legitimacy

HOW DO YOU EXPLAIN THE SIGNIFICANCE OF YOUR ACTION RESEARCH?

You are here in your action enquiry:

What is my concern?

Why am I concerned?

How do I show the situation it is and as it develops as I take action?

What can I do? What will I do?

How do I generate evidence from the data?

How do I check that any conclusions I come to are reasonably fair and accurate?

How do I explain the significance of my action research?

How do I modify my ideas and practices in light of my evaluation?

WHAT IS THE SIGNIFICANCE, OR IMPORTANCE, OF YOUR ACTION RESEARCH?

Remember that doing action research involves establishing the quality of your action and your research. This is important for the following reasons.

Why you should establish the quality of your action and your research

You aim to establish the quality of your action in terms of finding out whether you are contributing to the wellbeing of yourself and other people you are with. You consider what is going on, and whether you are living your values in your practice. If not, you take action to try to live your values more fully in your practice.

You aim to establish the quality of your research by demonstrating its methodological rigour: that is, you have fulfilled all the research steps that enable you to make a knowledge claim about how you have improved your practice. You may need to improve your capacity to do research, in which case you explain what you have done.

Why you should establish the significance of your action and your research

The action part of your action research is significant in that:

- It enables you to show how you have evaluated and improved aspects of your practice. This shows that you are exercising your professionalism as a caring and capable practitioner.

- It shows that you have a strong sense of accountability, both to your own integrity and to the wellbeing of your clients and students.

The research piece of your action research is significant in that:

- You show that you are capable of doing high quality research; you therefore rightly position yourself as a practitioner-researcher.

- You show that you have improved practice through creating knowledge. Your knowledge enables you to contribute to theory generation, i.e. you are saying that you both know what you are doing (you speak about knowledge) and you are able to explain what you are doing (you speak about theory).

WHY IS IT IMPORTANT THAT YOU SHOULD EXPLAIN THE SIGNIFICANCE OF YOUR ACTION RESEARCH?

Explaining the significance of your action

This is important because:

- You show that you are capable and authorised to speak as an expert practitioner. You know what you are doing as a professional and people can have confidence in you.

- You contribute to raising the status of your own profession. You are not a bunch of amateurs, but people who are deeply committed to practising in a professional way, and making their accounts of practice available for public scrutiny.

Explaining the significance of your research

This is important because:

- You demonstrate that you are capable of generating theory, that is, you are able to explain why you are practising in a particular way and what you hope to achieve. You can engage in debates about the way that your own work and the work of others in your profession should be judged and why it should be judged in this way.

- You are therefore developing new discourses and debates about how your profession may move forward, and what pathways it may take. You are professing your own commitments to high quality professionalism.

HOW ARTICULATING THE SIGNIFICANCE OF YOUR ACTION RESEARCH CAN GIVE IT LEGITIMACY

There is a big difference between the idea of validity and the idea of legitimacy. Validity is to do with matters of truthfulness, and legitimacy is to do with matters of power. For example, in recent years, some allegations of child abuse have not been taken seriously, or have been covered up by those in power. However, when investigated, the allegations have been demonstrated as valid. From a different perspective, some famous footballers (we know who you are), also in recent years, have won matches from handballs, as attested to by millions of people who saw the matches on television. These wins were granted legitimacy by referees, although those decisions were technically invalid because handballs break the rules of football. It is most important for you to show that you have tested the validity of your knowledge claims so that you can argue with confidence for their acceptance and legitimacy in the public domain.

EXAMPLE

My name is Don and I am the principal of a college of nursing. My background is in health care, and I have also undertaken management training. My action research question is always about how I can provide opportunities for trainee nursing staff to engage in their own professional development through action research. I find funding for them whenever possible, and I negotiate time for them to do their studies. This means I have to be creative about managing budgets and time schedules, but I succeed in managing things because I am deeply committed to the ongoing professionalisation of the nursing profession. I am proud of what I do, as I feel I am contributing to nurses' sense of wellbeing, which, I hope, will communicate to patients. I also hope that I encourage the nurses themselves to have the confidence to say why they feel their work is important, and how it is contributing to the patients' and their own sense of wellbeing. I believe it is important for all of us to be able to say why we do what we do, and to say why it is important. If we can't speak for ourselves, who will? And if we can't articulate the reasons and purposes for what we are doing, we cannot expect other people to do so. I am pleased that our college is a place where everyone can feel valued and valuable, and this makes my work and life worthwhile.

EXERCISE

Imagine that you are on the national board for your profession, and that you are acting in the role of expert adviser. What recommendations would you make for the future development of your profession?

Why would you make these recommendations?

Where would you base your judgements? What kind of evidence would you produce to show that your recommendations were justified?

How would you argue your case in the face of possible opposition from people who wish to retain the status quo?

Would you be able to take on such a role? Would you be prepared to do so?

REFLECTIVE QUESTIONS

Think of these questions:

- ✓ Are you clear about the significance of what you have done in your action research? Can you explain this significance?

- ✓ Why is it important to be able to do so?

- ✓ Can you explain how your action research has validity?

- ✓ Can you explain why people should listen to you and take your ideas seriously, and so grant you legitimacy?

SUMMARY

This section has set out ideas about the importance of explaining in what way your action research is significant and why people should take your work seriously. It has outlined ides about why both your action and your research are important, and how your articulation of their significance can contribute to new practices and new thinking in the field.

So you have almost completed the first action reflection cycle. What have you learned? What have you stopped doing? What have you started doing differently? These issues are dealt with in the next chapter.

Chapter 21
How do I modify my ideas and practices in light of my evaluation?

This chapter sets out ideas about how to think about continuing your action enquiry. It makes the point that action research is both about doing projects and also about developing an enquiring and optimistic attitude to life.

The chapter contains ideas about these issues.

- How do I modify my ideas and practices in light of my evaluation?
- Where are you now?
- Where are you going?
- How are you going to get there?

HOW DO I MODIFY MY IDEAS AND PRACTICES IN LIGHT OF MY EVALUATION?

You are here in your action enquiry:

What is my concern?

Why am I concerned?

How do I show the situation as it is and as it develops as I take action?

What can I do? What will I do?

How do I generate evidence from the data?

How do I check that any conclusions I come to are reasonably fair and accurate?

How do I explain the significance of my action research?

How do I modify my ideas and practices in light of my evaluation?

WHERE ARE YOU NOW?

At this point, you have completed one action-reflection cycle. You have carried out an action research project that has helped you to evaluate a particular aspect of your practice, and improve it as appropriate. You are also able to say how and why you have done so, and stand over your claims with authority.

However, although you have come to the end of one action-reflection cycle, this does not mean that your enquiry is finished. Far from it, because you have probably unearthed more issues than you had anticipated. This is to be expected. As long as we live, life is going to be interesting and problematic. You are probably never going to get to a situation where everything is perfect, and everything you believe in actually does happen. As long as you are alive, new challenges and opportunities will emerge.

WHERE ARE YOU GOING?

This is what makes action research so exciting. We saw in Chapter 6 that in traditional research you walk along a predetermined pathway, expecting to find a concrete answer. Although this kind of research may be appropriate for scientific enquiry, it is often not helpful in making sense of real-life issues, where concrete answers are seldom forthcoming, and, even if they do emerge, are short-term and unstable. Life is full of risk and uncertainty. Doing anything is an act of faith. This is an important idea that may help you get to where you would like to be.

HOW ARE YOU GOING TO GET THERE?

It is important always to have faith – in other people, in yourself, in your God. It is important to know that life continues. Even when terrible things happen, life finds a way, and continues. Getting through the day is often a case of putting one foot in front of the other.

Life is for celebrating, wherever and whenever possible, not for struggling through. We know, of course, that millions of people have no option but to struggle. For those of us who are privileged enough to be able to speak and act for ourselves, it is our responsibility to use our knowledge to enable all people to celebrate life, to make their contributions in ways that are right for them, and to feel valued and valuable.

The research methodology that most suits this attitude is action research. It is more than a methodology, more a philosophy. We should all adopt enquiring attitudes, and ask, 'How do I do what I would like to do? How do I improve the quality of my own life and work, and enable others to do the same? How do I celebrate the good in terms of my values? How do I justify my ideas and work in light of public critique?'

No one can force you to do this. It is your choice, and your choices are your own. Just make sure you choose well, and can hold yourself accountable for what you choose.

EXAMPLE

My name is Anne and I am an alcoholic. I have been an alcoholic for twenty years. I have actually stopped drinking, but I am still an alcoholic because I think about having a drink all the time and I have to exercise discipline not to take the next drink. I stopped drinking because I became ill and was hospitalised, and the doctors warned me then that I was heading for disaster. They advised me to do all sorts of things as a form of therapy, including returning to study. So I did. I am now embarked on a professional development course to try to gain some extra qualifications that will enable me to find and hold down a job. The course I enrolled on required me to do an action research project. I have completed one action reflection cycle, and my task is now to write a reflective essay to say what I have learned from the experience of doing the course and if I have changed my thinking or practices. I can definitely say what I have learned and what I have changed. I have learned to have patience with other people and with myself. I have learned to step back and look at myself with a critical eye, and to review my own thinking. I have learned to value myself for who I am and what I know. I have definitely modified my ideas and practices since I began the project. I can show you evidence of the early days, when I was stumbling around the ideas of creating my own knowledge. Now I am confident that I have created new knowledge, mainly of myself. I imagine I will always be an alcoholic – once an alcoholic, always an alcoholic. But I now know how to control it, and how not to let the drink control me. A full bottle remains on the shelf. I have faith that it will remain there.

EXERCISE

Do the following:

Draw a diagram to show the journey you have taken through your action research. Show where you have come from and where you are going, and also how you hope to get there. Make sure you indicate how your learning has developed, and how this has influenced the actions you have taken in order to try to influence other people's learning as well as continue to influence your own.

REFLECTIVE QUESTIONS

Please reflect on the following questions:

✓ How do you feel about your first action enquiry? Do you think it was successful? Did you achieve what you set out to achieve? Did things go as you expected?

✓ Could you have done things differently? Or better? How?

✓ Has your first action reflection cycle led to new insights? How can you develop them?

✓ Will you continue your action enquiry into new cycles? How?

✓ How are you going to record these processes?

SUMMARY

This section emphasises the need for you to see your action enquiry as an ongoing, lifelong programme of enquiry. It is important to see the end of your enquiry as the beginning of the next. It is a time for reflecting on what went well, and what could perhaps change next time round, to plan for future enquiries and ways to contribute to the betterment of the quality of living for all people, including yourself.

This now brings you to the end of the first cycle of your action research project, and you are ready to continue with new cycles of action and reflection. The next part of this book discusses some of the possible implications of what you have done for your own personal and professional development, and how this may contribute to the professional education of others.

PART 4

WHAT IS THE SIGNIFICANCE OF MY ACTION RESEARCH? WHAT ARE THE POSSIBLE IMPLICATIONS?

This part is about the significance of your action research, and sets out some potential implications. It contains Chapters 22, 23, 24 and 25.

Chapter 22 speaks about some implications for your personal and professional development.

Chapter 23 considers some possible implications for whole organisational development.

Chapter 24 is about your potential contribution to the development of good social orders.

Chapter 25 deals with some implications of your action research for new ways of thinking (logics) and new ways of knowing (epistemologies).

Each chapter shows the relationship between doing your action research and your contributions to personal and professional development and wellbeing, at individual, systemic and social levels. An argument is made throughout that the power of one individual doing their action research has the potential to influence world orders.

Chapter 22

Implications for your personal and professional development

This chapter discusses some implications of your action research. It makes the point that you need to tell your story to show how you hold yourself accountable for what you are doing. This will enable you to contribute to a body of knowledge that will help other people learn how to do the same. The chapter contains the following.

- Implications of your action research for your own personal and professional development

- Making the implicit explicit

- Developing the capacity for critique

- Action research for moral accountability

IMPLICATIONS OF YOUR ACTION RESEARCH FOR YOUR OWN PERSONAL AND PROFESSIONAL DEVELOPMENT

You have done your action research. So what?

The implications of what you have done are enormous, including:

- You have taken control of your own learning and practice.

- You have shown that you are a competent and capable practitioner who can make decisions for yourself.

- You have got on the inside of ideas to do with research and theory; you have theorised your practice.

- You have developed the capacity to speak for yourself, and you can say why it is important to do so.

Doing this has involved energetic consciousness raising and self-appraisal. It has also involved making explicit what is already implicit.

MAKING THE IMPLICIT EXPLICIT

The process of making explicit what is already implicit goes like this:

- I decide to become more aware of what and how I am doing things.

- This helps me to understand the situation I am in more clearly.

- My improved understanding helps me evaluate my work and change it as necessary. I begin asking questions about the kinds of influence I am having on myself and on those I am working with.

- I make judgements about whether the changes I am making are helping the people I am working with. I do this by checking my perceptions with theirs.

- I change my way of working again in light of their perceptions, and we negotiate how we will be together.

- Our agreement to work together helps us improve the quality of work and living for us all.

Learning how to improve your learning and practice therefore is not just about investigating what you are doing but involves developing increased awareness of why you are doing it and what you hope to achieve. This comes mainly through developing the capacity for critique.

DEVELOPING THE CAPACITY FOR CRITIQUE

People often confuse the words 'criticism' and 'critique'. 'Criticism' tends to imply that someone is doing something wrong, and their errors are pointed out to them. Errors are then seen as 'bad', though this is not necessarily the case. Errors are in fact part of trying to live a good life, where sometimes things go as you wish and sometimes not. Criticism of this kind is often (though not always) negative, and tends to be linked with the need to develop greater insight.

'Critique', on the other hand, is essential for helping you to see and question what is going on so you can find ways to improve it. Self-critique is probably the hardest discipline to develop. We tend not to question what is going on in our lives or our thinking, and we get into the habit of accepting things as they are, including our non-questioning ways of thinking. Bourdieu (1992) describes this situation as like a fish that does not know it is in water.

However, when we begin asking questions about how we can improve things, new critical awareness can develop, and new thinking and practices emerge. Critique means stepping outside yourself, looking at yourself as a stranger, and asking, 'Am I doing what I should be doing?', and finding ways of doing so.

ACTION RESEARCH FOR MORAL ACCOUNTABILITY

Doing your action research then becomes a way of showing how you hold yourself accountable for how you choose to live and work. You accept the responsibility of your own actions before trying to influence other people's thinking and actions. You know you cannot accept responsibility for other people's thinking and actions, but you can, and must, accept responsibility for your own. However, it is not enough just to talk about these ideas: we also need to show that we are doing them, so that the ideas become real. Here is an example of what this can look like.

EXAMPLE

My name is Abdul and I work as a newspaper editor. As editor, I am responsible for the work of the other journalists who work on my paper. I have always been aware of the need to interrogate the stories I hear, and write fact-based but critical accounts for the public. I believe it is the responsibility of journalists to contribute to the education of the public by telling the truth, even though this may sometimes be uncomfortable for them.

As an editor I understand that it is my responsibility to encourage the newspaper staff to become critical, so that they can make informed decisions about how they write about the events they observe. I encourage all staff to undertake their action enquiries into their practices as journalists, and I encourage them to make themselves activist agents in real-life situations. However, if they are to do this successfully they need first to explain how they make themselves critical, otherwise they could be seen as phoney.

I have developed the strategy of setting aside time at our weekly staff meetings for colleagues to explain to others how they continually question their assumptions, and make themselves aware of any implications. I encourage them to write their stories and share them with colleagues. I also make space in the paper for one journalist per week to publish their account of practice, so the public can see whose voice they are listening to. So two sets of stories are being told at the same time. The first set is the stories of the journalists as they learn with and from one another, and maintain their capacity to be critical; and the second set is the stories they report on. These two sets of stories become the newspaper archives, and they are all in the public domain.

I believe that the case studies of the journalists form a vital body of knowledge that has the potential to inform the profession of journalism. It shows the power of individuals when they improve their capacity to speak critically. I would say that what I am doing, as a newspaper editor, is providing a powerful opportunity for professional development of a kind that is easily within reach of every practitioner. Each person can contribute to new thinking and practices in their profession, as well as enhance its status; their work moves from the carrying out of everyday actions to research-based professionalism.

REFLECTIVE QUESTIONS

Ask yourself the following:

✓ Have I the capacity for personal critique? Do I exercise it?

✓ Can I show that I hold myself morally accountable for what I do?

✓ Can I produce evidence to show these processes in action? If so, what kind of evidence would I produce?

SUMMARY

This chapter has outlined some implications of doing your action research, to do with how you have developed the capacity to think and act for yourself. It has emphasised the need for self-critique as the basis of personal learning and professional development. Stories that show this process in action can form a powerful knowledge base that could inform new thinking and practices for others in the profession.

In the next chapter we consider how these ideas can contribute to whole organisational development.

Chapter 23
Implications for whole organisational development

This chapter is about how your action research can contribute to whole organisational development. It makes the point that individuals create and sustain their organisational cultures, so they must be vigilant that those cultures are the ones they want, otherwise they should change them.

The chapter contains these ideas.

- Action research and whole organisational development
- Individuals and organisational cultures
- How professional learning is managed
- Managing the contexts of professional learning

ACTION RESEARCH AND WHOLE ORGANISATIONAL DEVELOPMENT

Doing action research means that you investigate your practice, evaluate whether it is satisfactory, and find ways to improve any aspects that need attention. However, you never do action research alone; you always act collaboratively with others, and all are open to their own learning through self-critique. Action research therefore becomes something people do to improve the quality of life for themselves and others.

This idea is key for organisational development. Each individual in an organisation can undertake their personal enquiry, or groups of individuals can identify a common interest and work collectively to address it, so they improve what they are doing individually and collectively.

It is, of course, risky, because you may find that your work is judged as not satisfactory, either by yourself or others. You may then need to make difficult decisions about whether or not to continue your enquiry, given that it may become uncomfortable; and it may also involve challenging decisions or remaining silent in the interests of a quiet life.

INDIVIDUALS AND ORGANISATIONAL CULTURES

Important here is the relationship between the individual and the organisation. Traditionally organisations are seen as having established structures, practices and ways of thinking. Put together, these form a culture, or system of social practices, 'the way things are done around here'. Often people come to believe that the culture is fixed and may not be changed. Habermas (1975) made the point that people create their own systems, but then tend to become complacent and fall asleep. While they are sleeping, the system somehow rises above their heads and takes on a life of its own. With luck, people wake up to what is happening; but too often they stay asleep and say things like, 'It's the system. We can't change it.' They forget that the system they created in the first place can be undone and recreated. This is when the self-critique of action research can be central in organisational renewal by encouraging individuals to develop their professional learning and their capacity to challenge assumptions.

However, two important issues arise:

* How professional learning is managed
* How the contexts of professional learning are managed

HOW PROFESSIONAL LEARNING IS MANAGED

The growing popularity of action research has triggered big changes in the management of professional learning, which are different from traditional approaches, as follows.

Traditional approaches

Traditional professional development approaches tend to work from

* A subject focus: the aim is to enable practitioners to develop subject or content knowledge;
* An advisory perspective: a subject adviser, who is an acknowledged expert in the field, offers support.

The underpinning assumptions of these approaches are that

* Knowledge is a 'thing' that exists inside the head of a knower, usually the subject adviser;
* The practitioner does not know, and needs to be told;
* Once told, the practitioner will apply the subject adviser's knowledge to their own practice.

Action research approaches

In action research approaches, professional development tends to work from

- A practice base, to enable practitioners to develop and refine knowledge of their practices;

- A consultative perspective, to develop a collaborative partnership between supporter and practitioner.

The underpinning assumptions of action research approaches are that

- Knowledge is a creative process of ongoing learning, and is grounded in practice;

- Practitioners know what they are doing, and can benefit from the advice and insights of others;

- Practitioners learn from one another, including through sharing accounts of their practices.

MANAGING THE CONTEXTS OF PROFESSIONAL LEARNING

Supporting professional development through action research is therefore grounded in a model of collaborative learning, where practitioners develop new ways of working while drawing on their own and others' experience and subject knowledge. Improving professionalism happens through ongoing personal action enquiry, not necessarily through the application of transmitted advice. New collaborative cultures of enquiry can be developed that will contribute to the education of all participants.

Some problematics

However, these approaches can be problematic. Supporters need high levels of interpersonal, counselling and pastoral skills, as well as in-depth subject knowledge, and this can often be difficult. They also need to be aware of the relationships between practitioners and organisational systems, especially when tensions arise between the practitioner's values and the organisation's values.

There are implications too for the relationships between the practitioner and the supporter. Traditionally, there is often a hierarchical power relationship between them: this is not usually educational for either party. In action research approaches, it is possible to build a genuine sense of partnership, a dialogue of equals, where both parties appreciate that each has a different role and level of expertise, but they are equal in personal and professional value.

The development of these understandings, and how circles of influence may be created, can lead to systemic improvement. It also becomes obvious how one person's action research can influence whole organisational development.

EXAMPLE

My name is Anne-Louise and I am the manager of a ski resort. Local businesses and business schools often send us trainee managers for on-the-job training. Until recently, our training practices took the form of lectures and seminars, where trainees learned about the principles and practices of managing a ski resort. One of our senior employees, however, took part in a higher degree programme for business management, and in turn he introduced us to the idea of action research.

He said that, as well as giving trainees lectures in how to manage a resort, we also ought to insist that they investigate for themselves how to manage one. This would involve speaking with skiers, going out on ski-runs themselves, considering the advantages of snow-mobiles over quad-bikes through trying them out, and so on – in other words, valuing their practice-based learning as much as their conceptual learning. We introduced this system, and suddenly found ourselves inundated with requests from our providing institutions to take more and more trainee managers. We were initially concerned that this simply meant that the trainees were having fun but not adding anything to improving their on-the-job learning. However, their evaluations on returning to their home institutions contained their positive reflections about being active in their own learning and how our course had relevance for their practice. The increased numbers naturally meant a boost of income for us. Action research has more advantages than one!

REFLECTIVE QUESTIONS

Ask yourself these questions:

- ✓ How do I feel about my capacity to influence organisational systems? Or should I stay quiet? What would happen in either case?

- ✓ How do I develop my professional learning? Do I rely on someone else to tell me what to do, or am I creative and proactive in imagining what to do?

- ✓ How do I relate to my colleagues? How do I relate to managers and professional developers? How do we manage our relationships?

- ✓ Do I see the potential of my action enquiry to influence processes of systemic change and improvement?

SUMMARY

This chapter has explored ideas about whole organisational development. It has made a case for your capacity to influence processes of organisational change and improvement. You are not separate from 'the system' but are part of it, and therefore well placed to influence it. You need to be aware of professional relationships, and become critical yourself of your own practice as the basis for the development of organisational cultures of enquiry.

The next chapter explores how these ideas can be transferred to new debates about social evolution, as well as the development of new public spheres that encourage us to think about how we can create the kind of society we wish to live in.

Chapter 24

Your contribution to good social orders

This chapter explores ideas about how your action enquiry enables you to contribute to good social orders. Because people always live in relationship with one another and with the planet, your action research can influence everyone's sense of wellbeing.

The section contains the following.

- Action research and good social orders

- The interconnected and generative transformational nature of all things

- The potential influence of your action research

- Developing new public spheres for informed debate

- Having faith in others and yourself

ACTION RESEARCH AND GOOD SOCIAL ORDERS

Ideas about whole organisational development apply also to influencing processes of social evolution and the development of good social orders. The central idea is that by doing action research you can show how you hold yourself accountable for your practices.

Think again about the generative transformational nature of evolutionary processes, and the interconnectedness of all things: if we are prepared to be publicly accountable, we develop a relationship of responsible connectivity with other people and with our planet. If so, what does it mean for you?

THE INTERCONNECTED AND GENERATIVE TRANSFORMATIONAL NATURE OF ALL THINGS

Imagine any garden you have been in. The garden probably has a range of plants – flowers, trees and weeds. Each plant is in a process of growth, always in a situation of transformational emergence. Even processes of decay are realisations of the emergent property of living phenomena. Taken all together, the plants form a living body of emergence.

Now think about what keeps the plants in a state of emergence: for example, the quality of air, soil and rain. The plants in turn influence the quality of their nurturing systems: as they decay, they become part of the soil that regenerates them. We are in a biosphere, an ecological system, where all aspects influence the growth of all other aspects.

The same happens with people and the social systems they create. Each individual may contribute to the evolution of another; collectives of individuals may contribute to other collectives. No one is separate from the other; all are interconnected and mutually influential. Similarly, their cultures and systems are also interconnected and mutually influential.

The patterns of influence are apparent in real-time – what happens in one part of the world influences what happens elsewhere; and they also happen through history – what happens at one point in time influences what happens in the future. Also, what we think may happen in the future influences what we do now. Nothing exists in isolation, and nothing comes into being in isolation. Everything is interconnected.

THE POTENTIAL INFLUENCE OF YOUR ACTION RESEARCH

You are a piece of all this. Whatever you do has potential influence in other people's lives. If you plant a flower in your garden, it contributes to the wider wellbeing of the planet. If you are at peace with yourself, you contribute to the wider peace.

Therefore, when you do your action research, you expect that other people will also do theirs. When you ask, 'How do I improve what I am doing?' there is an assumption that you are doing this for another as well as yourself. There is also an assumption that the other will reciprocate, so a relationship of mutual care and responsibility evolves. This can influence the development of new kinds of public spheres for informed debate.

DEVELOPING NEW PUBLIC SPHERES FOR INFORMED DEBATE

A public sphere is a place where people can meet and debate issues that are important to them. Too often contemporary public spheres are dominated by the loudest voices. Through doing your action research and making your findings public, you can influence the development of new kinds of public sphere where every voice may be heard. Those who are entitled to speak are the ones who show how they hold themselves accountable for what they are doing. Doing your action research entitles you to speak with your own voice, to tell your truth as you understand it. Further, according to Foucault (2001), it is your responsibility to speak your truth, to challenge normative assumptions and encourage others also to develop their capacity for self-critique.

However, it has to be understood that people do not always share the same values, and some distance themselves from others. Some are self-serving and greedy for money and power. How do you cope with potential hostility and a refusal to engage?

HAVING FAITH IN OTHERS AND YOURSELF

Your answer is to continue to have faith in others and in yourself. You have faith that you can influence others' thinking and actions through showing how you are growing through your action enquiry. You also need to remember that you cannot, and should not try to accept responsibility for what other people are thinking and doing. Your task is to accept responsibility for what you are thinking and doing, and try to influence others (but not force them) to do the same.

Perhaps your most powerful resource is faith in yourself. Many people say that no one person can significantly influence social transformation. This is not necessarily so. First, we have to believe that it is possible to improve things, otherwise we may as well give up altogether on every effort to improve the quality of living – medical research, adventure and exploration, educational and social programmes. If we live in hope, at least we have some notion of how we can create the kind of society we wish to live in. If we do not try, we can be sure of a zero outcome.

If you can make your action enquiry public, and produce an account to show how you tried to improve one small aspect of your work, you stand some hope of influencing the thinking of someone somewhere, so that they too will try to do something similar in their own context.

It is always worth trying, so you should go ahead and try. Dare to dream, and then make the dream come true.

EXAMPLE

My name is Gavin Foury, and I am a white male attorney in Cape Town. I want to tell you about my recollection of my great hero, Nelson Mandela, who, like many other people throughout history, was imprisoned for his commitments to fighting for democracy and freedom. He was released in 1990, after serving twenty-seven years in prison. In 1994, he became the first President of the new democratic South Africa.

At that time, we whites were anxious about what would happen when democracy broke out. We had visions of what had happened elsewhere, where the white minority who had formerly been in power were attacked, and some killed. We feared a bloodbath; and many people, not prepared to take the risk, had sold up and left for more secure places. Those of us who stayed did so because we believed in the possibility of a brave new world.

In the event, Nelson Mandela showed us all how to live well. He called for peace and reconciliation among all groups, and led the way by demonstrating kindness to those who had previously been his oppressors. Through his individual example, a country was transformed.

My enduring memory of the dismantling of Apartheid was that one morning my wife, sons and I went to the beach that had previously been reserved for us whites. There we saw some black people, standing up to their ankles in the ocean, gazing around quietly and with dignity. They offered a tentative smile when they saw us on what was now our – our – beach. I smiled tentatively in return, and with a sense that something was irrevocably changed for ever.

REFLECTIVE QUESTIONS

Think about these questions.

- ✓ Do you see the connections between your action research and wider social evolution? Can you explain what those connections are?

- ✓ Do you see the potentials of your action research for influencing other people's learning? How?

- ✓ Do you know a story about how one person influenced a wider group, or a social order? Think of Gandhi, Stalin and Jesus. What stories are told about them? What kind of story will be told about you?

SUMMARY

This section has explored ideas to do with possible implications of your action research for the creation of good social orders. It has drawn this relationship from an understanding of the interconnected and generative transformational nature of all things. You are encouraged to think about how telling your story will influence other people's learning for the good.

This chapter has considered how you can contribute to new ways of purposeful acting. However, purposeful acting is always grounded in thinking, so it becomes not only a matter of influencing what people do, but also of finding ways of influencing how they think. This is the focus of the next chapter.

Chapter 25

Some implications of your action research for new ways of thinking (logics) and new ways of knowing (epistemologies)

This chapter is more advanced than others, but aim to work with it, because appreciating the ideas would greatly enrich your understanding of what you are doing. It is about the need to develop new ways of thinking (logics) in order to inform new ways of knowing (epistemologies) that can potentially transform social practices and contribute to sustainable wellbeing. It deals with the following issues.

- The idea of a new epistemology
- The differences between traditional and new epistemologies
- How your action research can contribute to the development of new epistemologies

THE IDEA OF A NEW EPISTEMOLOGY

Technically, the word 'epistemology' means a theory of knowledge, including a theory of knowledge acquisition or knowledge creation. It means, in simple terms, 'what is known and how it comes to be known'. When you speak about your action research you say, 'I know what I know and I know how I have come to know it.' This is especially important when you speak about how you have improved your practice. You say, 'I know that I have improved my practice, and I know how I have done so.' In other words, you say you can offer descriptions and explanations for what you have done and are doing: you can theorise your practice.

   Bear in mind that what you know and how you come to know it (your epistemology) depends on how you think about things, and how you choose to think about things. How we think is referred to as our logics; and how we choose to think involves our values. So if what we do is informed by how we think, then improving practice begins with improving thinking. You ask, how do I need to think in order to understand and improve my practices?

THE DIFFERENCES BETWEEN TRADITIONAL AND NEW EPISTEMOLOGIES

The epistemological underpinnings of traditional research and action research are different, because their logics and values are different.

Action research is grounded in relational and transformational ways of knowing (epistemologies), and in relational and transformational ways of thinking (logics). These ways are always changing because the connectedness of all things inevitably transforms relationships throughout the entire ecology. Everything is understood as containing the potentials for unlimited possibilities, all connected.

This is different from traditional research, where it is supposed that a straight line of enquiry will show a cause and effect relationship (if I do this, that will happen), and will also lead to a direct and final answer. The epistemologies that inform traditional research are linear and fragmented: they go direct from A to Z, without any twists or turns.

Action research does not aim for final answers, because any answers immediately transform into new questions. Action research is therefore a powerful methodology of change because nothing is seen as static or unchanging. Through doing your action research you are able to give explanations for how and why things change, including you, even as you and they are changing. Everything, including yourself and your thinking, is connected and open to change and improvement.

HOW YOUR ACTION RESEARCH CAN CONTRIBUTE TO THE DEVELOPMENT OF NEW EPISTEMOLOGIES

These ideas have implications for the future wellbeing of ourselves and our planet. It therefore becomes the responsibility of action researchers to develop new epistemologies for all fields of enquiry, especially within the following priority areas:

* Developing ecological awareness
* Developing environmental awareness
* Developing awareness of human and animal rights

Developing ecological awareness

There is a strong relationship between what you do and human, animal and planetary wellbeing: as, for example, when you ask, 'How do I encourage my customers to purchase Fair Trade goods?' or 'How do I ensure fair management practices in my organisation?' Through engaging with these kinds of questions, and making your findings public, you show how you can potentially influence wider spheres. The development of your own ecological awareness enables you to see the potential influences of your action research through space and time.

Developing environmental awareness

An enormously important issue is the need to protect the environment. Everyone speaks about cutting emissions and the use of natural resources by 2050, otherwise the world will be in danger. This is nonsense. If we continue using the world's resources without putting them back there will be no world in 2050 to save.

You can undertake your action enquiry into how you can help others, such as your students and clients, to conserve natural resources: or find more environmentally friendly ways of packaging goods, or re-use materials; or develop other forms of energy and fuels to light homes and run cars. Not much action research has been done in this area, and not many published accounts are available. You can produce your report and put it into the public domain, and gain a foothold in the field that will influence new thinking and new practices.

Developing awareness of human and animal rights

Equally essential is the need to protect humans and other animals. This involves recognising that all living creatures are connected in a range of ways, and that we all potentially influence one another through what we say and do.

Ways of knowing (epistemologies) that see everyone connected with everyone else also see people as equal in worth and status. In their natural state, all babies have equal status, and so do corpses. It is only when they are positioned within hierarchical social systems that their status changes. Some babies are born in rich and comfortable households, and some are born in fields. Some corpses are buried with pomp and ceremony, and some are ignored at roadsides.

Your action research can influence the thinking that allows babies to be born in fields and die; and that allows corpses to be abandoned at roadsides. Your action research demonstrates respect for all life forms, in all contexts, as equal in worth, status and prestige. Personal circumstances have nothing to do with personal worth. You can explain how this belief inspires your action research.

EXAMPLE

My name is René and I am an aid worker in places of intractable conflict. Every minute I see what perpetual war does to people. I also see why war is allowed to continue. The mentality that allows wars to continue is grounded in traditional epistemologies that see things, including people, as separate and organised into hierarchies of status. I do not see people as separate, or any one person as better than another.

I am currently enrolled on a professional development course, where I am required to write an account of my action research. I emphasise the transformational nature of my research methodology as I ask, 'How do I help people to help themselves?' This helps me to explain how I am enabling other people, as I do, to develop good relationships with one another, and with their planet.

REFLECTIVE QUESTIONS

Ask yourself the following questions.

✓ Have you thought through the relationships between all aspects of your action research? Please take a moment to write out the connections between:

- Your epistemology and your practice
- Your research and your research participants
- Your living theory and the people you are working with
- Your action research and the wellbeing of the planet
- Your action research and the future of children

✓ Can you articulate the relationship between your research question and your claim to knowledge? Consider, for example, how your question 'How do I contribute to children's wellbeing?' transforms into the claim, 'I have contributed to children's wellbeing.'

✓ Now ask yourself: Have I contributed to saving someone's life today? If you are doing your action research, you probably have.

SUMMARY

This chapter has outlined the idea that how we act is informed by how we think, so it is important to think in ways that are grounded in a view of the interconnectedness of all things. This means especially developing awareness of environmental issues and the rights of all living creatures to a full and happy life. Your action research can inform wider thinking about these issues and raise awareness of the relationship between research and sustainable wellbeing.

We now consider this issue: If you want to exercise your educational influence in other people's thinking, you need to produce a written report of some kind. If you want to convince people to take you and your action research seriously, you need to write a good quality report.

You can find advice on how to do this in the next Part.

PART 5

WRITING AND DISSEMINATING YOUR ACTION RESEARCH

This part is about writing up your action research and disseminating it in the public domain. It contains Chapters 26, 27, 28, 29, 30 and 31.

Chapter 26 gives advice about developing your writing skills and capacities.

Chapter 27 explains how to write an action research report.

Chapter 28 gives advice about writing a progress report.

Chapter 29 outlines how to write a proposal for a range of purposes.

Chapter 30 advises how to write for academic accreditation.

Chapter 31 is about compiling your professional portfolio.

The point is made throughout that successful writing involves developing many capacities: content knowledge (about action research), practice knowledge (showing that you can do action research), and writing knowledge (writing in a way that will hold the attention of your reader and gain you recognition). You can develop all these capacities with practice.

Chapter 26
Developing your writing skills and capacities

This chapter offers advice about general writing skills and the kinds of issues you need to think about. It contains the following.

* Researching writing
* Critical questions to guide your writing
* Developing your writing skills and capacities

RESEARCHING WRITING

Some people seem to have a natural talent for writing, while others struggle. One thing is for sure: all writers have to work at their craft. Good writing, like everything else worthwhile, takes a small amount of talent and a big amount of hard work.

Aim therefore to cultivate an appropriate attitude to your writing. Approach it with a sense of humbleness: you need to find ways to best maximise your chances of success. This means learning how to write, especially how to write for a specific market, and then producing a text that will keep that market wanting to read more.

Here are some ideas about how you can do this.

CRITICAL QUESTIONS TO GUIDE YOUR WRITING

For any piece of writing, ask yourself the following.

* Who are you writing the report for?

* Why are you writing it?

* What is its content? What do you want to say that no one else has said before?

* What else do you hope to communicate?

* What form will the report take?

Who are you writing the report for?

Think of the person who will read your report, and develop a sense of audience. Ask yourself, 'What does my reader want to read?' and then write in a way that is right for that reader (a manager does not want to read a report written for your critical friend). Keep focused on the person you have identified and write for them.

Why are you writing it?

You are writing to let people know about your action research, so aim to communicate a sense of purposefulness. You are writing to tell them what you have done, why you have done it, and why it is important that they should listen to you.

What is its content? What do you want to say that no one else has said before?

Which topics do you want to talk about? Ask yourself, 'Why should people want to read this?' Keep to the point and do not wander. If you are writing about your own practice, do not start writing about someone else's: if you are writing about beekeeping, do not talk about cats. Give an outline of your action research, emphasising what is original about it, i.e. that you have improved your practice and you can explain how and why you have done so.

What do you hope to communicate?

Aim to communicate that you are a competent and capable action researcher, whose ideas people should take seriously. You can do this by making sure that the content and form of your report and your style of writing are right for the job.

What form will the report take?

Your report should reflect the form of an action enquiry. Organise your ideas to show its cyclical form, from identifying a research issue and question: how you moved forward through asking critical questions; how you worked collaboratively with others and listened to their advice; how you gathered data and generated evidence in relation to specifically articulated criteria and standards ... and so on. Tell the story of what you did, making sure that you give descriptions (what you did) and explanations (why you did it).

DEVELOPING YOUR WRITING SKILLS AND CAPACITIES

Aim to develop your skills and capacities as a writer. Here are the main points to bear in mind.

Writing takes time and practice

Do not expect to become an expert writer overnight, or get it right immediately. Like everything, writing takes time and practice. Cater on about three complete drafts, often more, to produce a manuscript that will catch and keep a reader's attention. Even the most experienced writers spend ages on planning, writing and refining a text before submission. Producing high quality texts that people will want to read takes work.

Write for a reader

Many people make a fundamental error of writing for themselves. Do not do this. Always write for a reader. The only thing your reader knows about you is what they read on a page, so keep your writing simple, to the point, and clear. Remind your reader periodically where they are in your text. Structure your text so that they can see the ideas in sequence. It is your responsibility to ensure that your reader understands what you are saying, not their responsibility to work it out for themselves.

Do your market research

Check what is required for a certain audience before you write, including any assessment criteria. If you are submitting a text for publication check what the editors or publishers want. Respect any instructions about word length, style of referencing or layout. Find out what works, and then produce a text that fits the bill.

Style of language

Readers have limited time, so they want a text to be clear, to the point and without fuss. They also want something that speaks to their experience and context. Keep your text uncluttered by doing this:

- avoid repetition
- avoid exaggeration
- use one idea per sentence
- keep your paragraphs focused
- talk the language of your audience – academic, vernacular, dialogue, or whatever is appropriate

Structure your writing

Write a report with a clear pathway through it, so your reader can follow your arguments easily. Make it clear that the text has a beginning, middle and end. Use part and section headings as signposts, and use 'A', 'b' and 'c' headings to keep your reader focused. Introduce new ideas carefully: do not drop your reader into a discussion unprepared. Summaries can be helpful before moving to the next piece.

Produce a clean manuscript

A clean manuscript means you produce an error-free piece of work, well laid out and clean on the computer screen or sheet of paper. Producing an error-free document means meticulous proofreading.

Proofreading

Proofreading involves reading your manuscript repeatedly, to ensure it is error-free. Make sure:

- there are no spelling or typographical errors

- all headings are consistent

- all references in the text appear in the list of references, and their details match

- all sentences are grammatical

- chapter headings match the contents list

- ... and so on.

It is your responsibility to produce a clean manuscript. It is definitely not the responsibility of your reader to make allowances for you.

Managing your schedule

Set yourself a writing schedule, including targets to complete sections of the work, as well as the whole piece. Get on with it, and, once started, keep at it, and do a piece of writing each day, even if only for ten minutes. If you leave your text for more than a day you will lose touch with it and will waste time catching up with where you were.

These are some of the main issues in learning how to write. Further ideas can be found in the books referred to below.

EXAMPLES

In this Part you are recommended to look at real-life examples of good practice, as well as consult a range of books on how to write for publication.

You can see examples of successful action research reports on the following websites: http://www.jeanmcniff.com (Jean McNiff's website) and http://www.actionresearch.net (Jack Whithead's website). On both websites you will find texts produced by the authors themselves, as well as from practitioners whose studies they have supported.

Read the works over time. Note how the writers produce well-written action research accounts. Note their style of writing, how they present arguments, how they weave theoretical aspects with personal reflections. Learn from these texts, and think about why the accounts were judged successful. Each one is different. You too should aim to produce your original account that does justice to your talents as an action researcher and as a writer.

You can find advice on learning to write for publication in a range of books such as the following:

Herr, K. and Anderson, G. (2005) *The Action Research Dissertation*. London, Sage

McNiff, J. (2011) *Writing for Publication in Action Research*. Dorset, September Books.

McNiff, J. and Whitehead, J. (2009) *Doing and Writing Action Research*. London, Sage

Murray, R. (2006) *How to Write a Thesis*. Maidenhead, Open University Press

… and other authors.

REFLECTIVE QUESTIONS

Ask yourself the following.

✓ Am I prepared to do what it takes to produce a high quality text? What do I need to do?

✓ Who am I writing for? What do they want to know? What do I want to tell them?

✓ What is my writing schedule?

SUMMARY

This chapter has set out some key aspects of writing. It emphasises the main points of doing your market research, writing for an identified reader, and being prepared to spend time and energy in producing a high quality report.

The next chapter gives advice about writing an action research report.

Chapter 27
Writing an action research report

This chapter outlines some of the key features of an action research report, and explains how the content and form of action research reports are different from traditional research reports. It contains the following.

- Contents of an action research report
- Form of an action research report

CONTENTS OF AN ACTION RESEARCH REPORT

Your report needs to demonstrate the key characteristics of action research, which include these.

The report is written from an 'I' perspective

Traditional research reports tend to be written in the third person – 'the researcher did …'. In action research reports you write in the first person – 'I did …' or 'We did …'

The claim to knowledge is stated at the beginning

At the beginning of your report you say what you have learned from doing the research: for example, 'I have learned how to encourage colleagues to work more cooperatively'. This statement represents your claim to knowledge. However, this statement could be seen simply as your opinion, so you need to show that it is true. In research language this means that you need to demonstrate the validity of your claim.

The report shows the process of testing the validity of the claim

To test the validity (truthfulness) of your claim you do the following:

- You articulate your research issue and question. (As nurses, we would like to ensure a high quality of patient care: 'How do we ensure a high quality of patient care?')

- You articulate your values as your living criteria and standards of judgement. (We believe all patients should enjoy a high quality of care.)

- You say how you gathered data to show the situation as it was and as it developed. (We gathered data to show how we tried out new systems to improve the quality of patient care.)

- You say how you took action. (We encouraged the patients to get out of bed in the morning if they were well enough and put on their day clothes.)

- You explain how you generated evidence from the data and ensured its authenticity. This involved showing how your data demonstrated the living out of your values. (We have authenticated statements from the patients to say that they feel a greater sense of wellbeing when sitting out of bed in their day clothes.)

- You now show how your evidence backs up your claim. (Our evidence leads us to think that we are justified in claiming that we are ensuring a high level of patient care.)

- You invite feedback from critical peers on whether they believe your claim. (We aim to present our work to our board of managers to persuade them to initiate new systems of care that put patients in charge of their own recovery.)

The report shows how you improved your learning in order to improve your practice

The report gives an account of your project. You say what you did to improve your situation, and you report on how you monitored the action, gathered data and generated evidence about progress. You give an account of what you learned, and how you could improve things even better in future.

The report itself is self-reflective

The report shows that you do not take anything for granted. You reflect critically on what you have written (about the actions you took, and how you conducted the research), and on how you have written it (whether you communicate the dynamic nature of the research). You also reflect critically on whether

- you are communicating things so that your reader can understand what you are saying;

- you are presenting yourself as authentic;

- you explain things in a truthful way;

- you write in a thoughtful way that shows your capacity for self-critique and your openness to the critique of others;

- you demonstrate your understanding of contextual issues.

FORM OF AN ACTION RESEARCH REPORT

Your report should be written in a way that reflects your original action plan, as inspired by the question, 'How do I improve my practice?' (Whitehead 1989). Your original action plan transformed into a series of action steps, as follows:

- you identified a concern;

- said why this was a concern;

- imagined a solution;

- acted in the direction of the imagined solution;

- gathered data on an ongoing basis to show what the situation was like to begin with and how it developed over time;

- generated evidence from the data in order to ground the knowledge claim;

- made the knowledge claim and tested its validity;

- articulated the significance of the action research;

- and modified practice in light of the evaluation …

This constituted one cycle of action reflection, which you can now report on. An action research report should contain an account of at least one action reflection cycle.

To guide your research you transformed your action plan into a series of critical questions, like this:

- What is my concern?

- Why am I concerned?

- How do I show the situation as it is and as it develops as I take action?

- What can I do? What will I do?

- How will I generate evidence from the data?

- How will I check whether any conclusions I come to are reasonably fair and accurate?

- How will I explain the significance of my action research?

- How will I modify my ideas and practices in light of my evaluation?

These same questions can now act as guidelines for your report, if you wish, and can form section headings. You now write in the past tense, telling your research story. Here is how you can do it, with an example to show what it may look like in practice.

Outline of an action research report

What was my concern?

Say what your research issue was. Contextualise the study: say who you were, where you worked, and anything else that may help your reader locate you and your research issue.

> I work as a manager in a hospital. My concern was how to encourage people to work together collaboratively. I was concerned that some people were not as cooperative as they could be.

Why was I concerned?

Say what was going on that made you want to investigate the situation more deeply. State your research question, beginning 'How do I ...?'

> It is important that all people work cooperatively in a hospital, to ensure good relationships that will benefit patient care. My research question became, 'How do I encourage people to work together cooperatively?'

How did I show the situation as it was and as it developed as I took action?

Explain the kind of data you gathered to show the situation as it was, and as it developed when you took action. Say which techniques you used at different stages of the research.

> I wanted to check whether my management practices were contributing to good working relationships, so I videoed myself in action with colleagues, and also to show their attitudes to one another and to me. I surveyed key members of staff to check their perceptions of what was happening. After that, as my research progressed, I used a range of data gathering techniques to show what I did, and how attitudes changed, and how I possibly influenced new practices among the staff.

What could I do? What did I do?

Say what your options were, and what you decided to do.

> I consulted with people whose opinion I respected, to check what they thought about the situation, and how I could contribute to improving it. They offered really helpful advice about how I could enable staff to talk with one another and feel more valued. They suggested I put on a series of staff development days where people could talk freely about how they were managing their own work. I took their advice and did as they suggested. I also made sure that I visited with each member of staff at least once a week, to have a chat and see how they were getting on. I also arranged for a more centrally located staff room with free tea and coffee to encourage staff to come together informally.

How did I generate evidence from the data?

Explain how you identify your values as your living criteria and standards of judgement. Say how you searched your data to find instances of those values in action. Explain that those pieces of data came to stand as your evidence, to ground your knowledge claims.

> I took my values of cooperative working and mutual respect as my living criteria and standards of judgement. I searched my data for those pieces that showed whether cooperative working and mutual respect were happening (or not), and how I was possibly influencing the situation. I found pieces of data that showed, for example, people talking together in the new staff room. I found other data that showed that people asked others' opinion about, for example, the regime of care for patients, or how they could make relatives feel more at ease when visiting patients.

How did I check that any conclusions I came to were reasonably fair and accurate?

Explain how you carried out several validity checks:

• you built up an evidence base to ground your knowledge claim;

• you ensured that the evidence showed how your values were being lived in practice, and named your values as your living criteria;

• you invited the critical feedback of critical colleagues and validation groups on your emergent knowledge claims.

> I compiled an evidence base from the data to show that my values were being realised in my practice. I checked thoroughly to ensure that my evidence was sufficiently robust to present to a validation group. I convened a validation group and presented my work to them. They agreed in general terms that the research was proceeding well, and suggested I might gather further data from patients, to see whether they were benefiting from the improved relationships among the staff.

How do I explain the significance of my action research?

Explain what the significance of your action research is for your own learning and the possible learning of others, and how you are contributing to new public thinking and practices.

> I believe the main significance of my research lies in my capacity to have improved my own thinking, and to have contributed to the thinking of others in the hospital. I ground this claim in my evidence base that contains a review from patients saying that they appreciate how staff worked together for the benefit of the patients. I have disseminated my research findings to another group of managers who have expressed an interest in doing similar things in their own organisations.

How do I modify my ideas and practices in light of my evaluation?

Explain how your research is influencing the development of new thinking and new practices for yourself and others.

> Our management group are now working together to set up a research consortium to establish action research ways of working. We are linking our group with a national body on improving practice in hospitals in the interests of patient care. I can claim that my individual research, undertaken collaboratively with colleagues, is having systemic influence in organisational practices in hospitals.

REFLECTIVE QUESTIONS

As you write your report, ask yourself the following questions:

✓ Am I writing in a way that shows the process of an action enquiry?

✓ Does my report demonstrate the key features of action research?

✓ Have I given an account of at least one cycle of action reflection?

✓ Do I show my understanding of the principles and practices of action research, and how I am living these in my practice?

✓ Do I show how I have contributed to improving my situation? Do I explain my understanding of how and why I have done so?

✓ Do I show how I can develop my action enquiry?

SUMMARY

This chapter has outlined how to write an action research report. It has explained that action research reports are different from traditional research reports, and how they are different in content and form. It has also given an example of an action research report.

We now turn to how to write different kinds of reports. From the many kinds possible, we have selected only a few: progress reports, writing proposals, academic reports, and compiling professional portfolios. Here they are.

Chapter 28
Writing a progress report

This section is about writing a progress report, and makes suggestions about possible contents and form. It contains the following.

- What goes into a progress report?
- Writing a work-based progress report
- Writing an academic progress report

WHAT GOES INTO A PROGRESS REPORT?

If you are writing a progress report it means that you are probably doing a project or course where you have to report back to someone. The aim is to update them, show that you are on the right track, outline your findings so far, and indicate where your research is going.

The report could be for colleagues at work, for a validation group or a supervisor in higher education, or as an academic paper for a conference, and may be presented as a written document or orally. Who you are writing for will influence how you write the report and what goes into it. You would therefore use a form of language and writing appropriate for your identified reader.

Whoever you are writing for, keep your critical questions in mind and use them as a framework. You need not use your questions as section headings, though you can if you wish. Aim, however, to organise your writing to show the systematic and methodologically rigorous nature of your research, as well as its practical benefits.

Here are some ideas on writing a work-based report for colleagues.

WRITING A WORK-BASED PROGRESS REPORT

Your organisation has probably invested time and money in you, so they want to know whether they are getting good returns. They want to know things such as:

- Is your action research helping you to improve your practice? Are you going to bring added benefit to the organisation?

- Is your action research going to help others? Has it the potential to influence organisational practices?

- Should they continue investing in you? Would this help to achieve the organisation's aims?

The section headings below will help you engage with these questions when organising your material. Each is matched with an action research type of question. You can show how a work-based report can be understood also as an action research report.

Organising the report

Organise your section headings as follows.

Aim of the study (Action research question: What is my concern?)

Say what the study is about, and outline the background. Articulate your research question: for example:

- 'How do we integrate people with special needs into our organisation?'

- 'How do we maximise the use of new technology?'

The importance of the study (Action research question: Why was I concerned?)

Say why the topic is important to your organisation and why they should feel confident in supporting you. Outline your own values and the organisation's values (perhaps refer to the mission statement), and show how your research enables these values to be lived in practice. Why is it important to integrate people with special needs into your organisation? Why is it important to maximise the use of new technology?

Outline of the contexts (Action research question: How do I show the situation as it is and as it develops?)

Explain what your contexts are, and how you have gathered data to show the situation as it is at the beginning of your study, before you have taken action. Outline how you have organised your study: e.g who has been involved and the timelines. Explain how you have gathered data regularly, and what kind of data gathering techniques you have used. Reassure your audience that you have observed meticulous ethical conduct throughout.

Actions taken so far (Action research question: What have I done? What changes have I introduced? How have I monitored practice and gathered data?)

Say what actions you have taken, and if you think they are working. Explain how you have acted in accordance with your values, and have tried to influence people's thinking so that they, like you, have learned to become critical of what you are all doing. Continue to explain how you have monitored practice, and gathered data.

Findings so far (Action research question: What have I found out from the data? What have I learned? How do I generate evidence from the data?)

Outline what has happened in your project, as shown by your data, to help you evaluate your work. What do the data show? Do they show what you have done? or what you have learned? or what other people have done? or what they have learned? How do you know? What are the data telling you? Through interpreting and analysing the data, in relation to your identified criteria and standards of judgement (in the form of your values), have you generated evidence from the data that shows the living out of your values?

Testing the validity of your provisional claim(s) to knowledge (Action research question: How do I check that any conclusions I come to are reasonably fair and accurate?)

Outline your provisional findings. Say whether people with special needs have been integrated into the workforce, and how they and others feel about things. Say how new technology is being used (if it is). Be honest about how things are going, but emphasise that this is work in progress. Explain that you have consulted regularly with others and invited their critical feedback on your provisional findings.

Potential impact value (Action research question: How do I explain the potential significance of my action research?)

Say what the potential impact value of your research is for yourself and your organisation. Reassure your colleagues that their investment is worthwhile, and would they please consider investing further in your own and others' workplace learning. Emphasise that you are engaging in improving practice and also developing a research base to enhancing professionalism within the organisation.

Future directions (Action research question: How do I modify my ideas and practices in light of the evaluation?)

Indicate how the research could progress, and how it would continue to have benefit. Say how you are going to change your thinking or research design in light of your evaluation, and what you hope to achieve. Be honest about anything that may not be working, and explain how you will deal with it. Stay upbeat and optimistic about possibilities.

WRITING AN ACADEMIC PROGRESS REPORT

Organising your material to write an academic progress report can be similar to how you write a work-based report, and can use the same section headings. However, your audience is different: you write an academic progress report for your supervisor, or as a conference paper, so the language is different.

An academic progress report emphasises the methodological and epistemological elements of your study as much as the practical aspects, as outlined in the work-based report. It would therefore look like this.

- A statement of the research issue, and a formulation of the research question. (What is my concern? How do I engage with it?)

- An exploration of the values base of the project, and how these values are lived (or not) within the research contexts. How you have engaged with the relevant literatures and what your contribution might be to the field. (Why am I concerned?)

- An outline of your research design and methodology; the technicalities of monitoring practice and gathering data. (How do I show the situation as it is and as it develops?)

- A description of the actions you have taken so far, and an explanation for why you have done so; an outline of one or more cycles of action and reflection in light of the developing situation. (What could I do? What did I do?)

- An explanation of how you intend to generate (or have generated) evidence from the data in relation to your values as identified criteria and standards of judgement; testing the validity of the knowledge claim against the critical feedback of peers. (How do I check that any conclusions I come to are reasonably fair and accurate?)

- An indication of how your thinking and practice have possibly changed in light of your evaluation. (How do I modify my thinking and practices in light of my evaluation?)

- An explanation of what you see may be the key significances of your action research. (How do I explain the significance of my action research?)

EXAMPLE

Here is an example of how you could write a work-based progress report. The key points are given, and you are invited to expand them into a proper report.

Aim of the study
To maximise the use of new technology in our organisation.

Research question
How do we maximise the use of new technology in our organisation?

The importance of the study
Values around the need to maximise the use of new technology within a knowledge-creating economy; values around technological excellence.

Outline of the contexts
Technology not sufficiently used; lack of skills among workforce; need to contribute to economic wellbeing. Outline of plans to monitor practice and gather data around action plans for improvement.

Actions taken so far
Implementation of staff up-skilling programme; delegation of responsibilities to key members of staff; state-of-the-art technology purchased.

Findings so far
Greater enthusiasm for new technology among workforce; improved knowledge and confidence; greater participation.

Testing validity of findings
Regular staff meetings to check perceptions of progress and consolidation of findings; rigorous evaluation of project.

Potential impact value
Improved outcomes and performance; more knowledgeable workforce.

REFLECTIVE QUESTIONS

Think about these questions.

- ✓ Are you confident that you can produce a progress report for a specific audience?

- ✓ Do you appreciate the difference between a work-based progress report and an academic progress report?

- ✓ Are you clear about the need to show the systematic research base of a progress report, and why this is important?

SUMMARY

This chapter has outlined how to write a progress report for your workplace and for an academic audience. Potential structures for these reports are shown and the differences between the different types explained. An outline of a possible report is given, and you are invited to expand it into a full report.

The next chapter deals with writing a proposal for a range of contexts.

Chapter 29

Writing a proposal

This chapter deals with writing proposals. It sets out what you should think about when writing a proposal, and what one looks like. It contains the following ideas.

- How do you write a proposal?
- Writing a proposal for an action research project
- Writing a proposal for a conference paper

Throughout you should draw on ideas from Chapters 26, 27 and 28. In this chapter some further ideas about possible contents and layouts are offered.

HOW DO YOU WRITE A PROPOSAL?

You would write a proposal for a range of purposes, including:

- Permission to do an action research project
- Submitting an academic paper for a conference
- Bidding for funding

All follow the same layout, though the emphasis is different depending on the purpose of the proposal.

Things to bear in mind

When writing any kind of proposal, remember the following.

- You are writing to persuade/convince someone that what you hope to do is worthwhile.
- You are hoping to gain their moral, practical and possibly financial support.
- You are making a case for the possible benefits of your action research for other people's learning, as well as your own.

Writing a proposal is a fine discipline for focusing your thinking and keeping you on track. It can act as a blueprint for what you are hoping to do and how you will do it.

WRITING A PROPOSAL FOR AN ACTION RESEARCH PROJECT

Here are some ideas for a proposal for an action research project, or to ask permission to do one. Keep your critical questions in mind as your framework.

Structure your proposal like this:

Background to the research: What is my concern?

Set out your research focus and question. Say who you are and give a brief outline of your contexts. This helps your reader decide whether the project is sufficiently worthwhile to approve.

Why do I want to do this research? Why am I concerned? What values do I hold around this topic?

Say why you wish to do the research, and how it will potentially benefit yourself and your organisation. This gives your reader information about why the project is worthwhile. If you are writing a proposal for an academic context, say how you will engage with the literatures.

What do I hope to find out from this research? How do I show that my reasons for wishing to do the project are justified?

Say what you hope to find out, i.e. what new knowledge you hope to create. Map out the scope of your project. This gives an idea about whether or not it is feasible. Say what new contribution you hope to make to existing knowledge of the field.

When and where will I do the research? How will I show the situation as it is?

Give information about the practicalities of the research, where you will do it and when. This shows that you have thought through logistical aspects.

How will I design my research? How will I gather data to show the situation as it is? Who will be my participants? How will I ensure ethical conduct?

Outline your research design. Say who your participants will be, and how you will involve critical friends and validation groups. Say how you will monitor practice and gather data. Explain how you will maintain high ethical standards. This identifies the different people you will involve and how you will work with them.

How will I conduct the research? What can I do? What will I do?

Outline what actions you could take, and what you intend to do. This gives ideas about how you intend to proceed.

How will I keep track of the research process and its effects? How will I gather data and generate evidence to show the situation as it develops?

Outline your different data gathering methods over time. Say how you intend to generate evidence from the data. This explains how you intend to produce an evidence base to ground your knowledge claims.

How will I test the validity of my research claims? How will I check that any conclusions I come to are reasonably fair and accurate?

Say how you intend to consult with critical friends and set up validation groups. This shows that you are aware of the need for critical feedback and of the provisional nature of knowledge.

How will I explain the significance of my research?

Say what you think may be the significance of the research project. This shows your awareness that your research could be important and influential in a range of ways.

How will I do things differently? How will I modify my ideas and practices in light of my evaluation?

Say how you are using this phase of the research to map out the territory, and that the findings from this phase may influence new ongoing phases. This indicates that you are aware of the generative transformational influence of your action research.

WRITING A PROPOSAL FOR A CONFERENCE PAPER

Writing a proposal for a conference paper involves all the above, but is usually structured differently. Many conference organisers ask for proposals to be submitted using the following, or similar, form:

- Background to the topic
- Research questions/focus of the enquiry
- Research methods and/or mapping the literature
- Analytical and/or theoretical frame
- Research findings and/or contribution to knowledge

You can draw on the ideas above, and also focus on what is needed here, as follows.

Background to the topic

Give the background to the research, outlining what your concern was and why it was important for the context.

Research questions/focus of the enquiry

Articulate your research question, and say why it was important for the context and for generating new knowledge. Say how the question gave a focus to your enquiry (e.g. that you could try to realise your values in your practice).

Research methods and/or mapping the literature

Say how you designed your research, and why, in relation to who you involved and how you gathered data. Say how this linked with the existing literature around the topic and around the methodology.

Analytical and/or theoretical frame

Say that you chose an action research methodology, and why. Say how this enables you to analyse and interpret your data and generate evidence to ground your knowledge claims.

Research findings and/or contribution to knowledge

Outline your provisional findings, the significance of your research, and how it is potentially contributing to knowledge of the field. Say how you intend to continue your research.

BIDDING FOR FUNDING

You can draw on all the above when bidding for funding, and mix and match sections as suits your purposes.

A generic set of headings could be as follows.

Outline of proposed project

Say what the project is about. Articulate the research question. Say why the area is important.

Theoretical background

Say what has been done in the area so far (cite the literatures) and how your proposed research will contribute new knowledge to the field.

Research design and methodology

Say how you will conduct your research, including the following:

- **Participants**: who you will involve, and how.
- **Research design**: how you will conduct the research, including data gathering methods and outline of ethical considerations.
- **Timeline**: say how long your research will take; give a start and end date.
- **Resources**: say what resources you need to do the research.
- **Procedures**: say how you intend to take action, and why.
- **Analysis**: say how you hope to analyse your data and generate evidence.
- **Validation:** say how you intend to test the validity of emerging claims to knowledge.

Anticipated contribution to knowledge

Explain the significance of your research by stating that it can potentially contribute to new thinking and new practices; say how you intend to disseminate your findings.

Modification of practice

Say how you believe your proposed research programme will contribute to ongoing research, and outline any plans for the continuation and development of the ideas.

REFLECTIVE QUESTIONS

Ask yourself the following.

✓ Are you confident that you can produce a proposal for a given audience? Are you clear that you must use a language relevant to that audience?

✓ Are you sure that any proposal must show the systematic and rigorous nature of the proposed enquiry?

✓ A proposal is always about selling an idea. Have you done your market research into what your audience wants?

SUMMARY

This chapter has outlined different aspects of writing a proposal for different audiences. It indicates that you need to anticipate the needs of your audience, write to persuade them to support your action research, and communicate in such a way that they will endorse your proposal.

The next chapter develops the idea of writing an academic report, including in the form of a dissertation or thesis.

Chapter 30
Writing an academic report, dissertation or thesis

This chapter deals with writing for academic accreditation through action research. Reports for academic accreditation come in several forms: as an undergraduate report, a masters dissertation, and a doctoral thesis. Whichever level you choose, the expectations remain largely the same. The chapter contains the following:

- Expectations for an academic report
- Writing an academic report

EXPECTATIONS FOR AN ACADEMIC REPORT

For all academic reports, at all levels, you are expected to show that you have engaged in an action enquiry, which has enabled you to achieve the following criteria.

- You have undertaken at least one cycle of an action enquiry, and probably more
- You have improved some aspect of practice
- You have researched that practice
- You have made a claim to knowledge, and tested its validity

At masters level you are also expected to show that

- You have demonstrated critical engagement
- You have engaged with appropriate literatures
- You can analyse, interpret and critique findings and arguments, and apply these to the improvement of educational practice as appropriate
- You can write a scholarly report

At doctoral level you are also expected to show that

- You have made an original contribution to knowledge of the field (at masters level the contribution to knowledge need not be original)

- You have produced a text that contains material worthy of publication

Although the different levels are judged in terms of increasingly scholarly criteria and standards, it is still possible to use your framework of critical questions for the writing of them all.

WRITING AN ACADEMIC REPORT

You can use the same framework for writing your academic report as appears throughout this book.

You also need to show that you appreciate what is meant by some specific terms in academic writing in general, and action research in particular. These include:

Improvement

This idea is central to action research. Improvement does not necessarily mean that something is faulty. It is used more in relation to ongoing evaluation, where you check that something is as good as you want it to be. Even if something is already really good, you still try to improve it, like champion footballers.

Transformational processes

This term refers to ongoing growth and evolution, on the basis that nothing is ever complete or final and is always in process of transformation. In processes of action research one aspect transforms into another. This is not a causal relationship; it is a transformational relationship, because all things are connected and influence the growth of the other things in their contexts.

Conceptual frameworks

A concept is an idea, so the ideas that you use to frame your work are called your conceptual frameworks. They are linked strongly with your values base. Examples of conceptual frameworks are gender issues (linked perhaps with values of equity), power and knowledge (linked with justice and accountability), difference (linked with equality and recognition), resistance (linked with power struggles), and so on.

Methodological frameworks

A methodology refers to the entire way you plan and conduct your research – not to be confused with the word 'method'. A method is a technique used for a specific purpose, such as data gathering or analysis, whereas a methodology is grounded in a philosophy and view of yourself in relation with others. Your chosen methodology is action research. You should state in your report why you have chosen action research rather than another methodology; this shows you are exercising critical engagement.

Critical engagement

This means not taking things at face value. The more advanced your studies, the more you are expected to demonstrate critical engagement. Aim to show how you engage critically with your own thinking, by deconstructing your assumptions. For example, explain that you used to think that intelligence is a thing that only some people have but you have thought critically about it and now understand that intelligence, if it exists, can be demonstrated in many ways, not only intellectual. You should also engage critically with the thinking of other people in the literatures. Gould's (1992) *The Mismeasure of Man* shows how he engages with the idea of intelligence in a scholarly way.

Original contribution to knowledge of the field

We said at the beginning of this book that all research aimed to generate new knowledge. Through your action enquiry you can show that you have generated knowledge of your practice. You can offer your theory of practice – that is, you are able to say why you do what you do, and offer justification for what you are doing, and how other people can learn from your example.

EXAMPLES

Here are two websites where you can read many academic reports.

1   http://www.actionresearch.net

This is Jack Whitehead's website. It is one of the most influential action research websites in the world.

Here are some examples of academic reports.

Example 1
Jocelyn Jones (2008) *Thinking with stories of suffering: towards a living theory of response-ability.* PhD thesis, University of Bath.

Retrieved 1 August 2010 from http://www.actionresearch.net/living/ jocelynjonesphd.shtml. Jocelyn's thesis is about how she, as a social worker and academic practitioner, reflects on her experiences as the child of a World War II veteran and interviews with European ex-prisoners of war; and how she brings this learning to inform her current practices.

Example 2
Je Kan Adler-Collins (2008) *Developing an inclusional pedagogy of the unique: How do I clarify, live and explain my educational influences in my learning as I pedagogise my healing nurse curriculum in a Japanese University?* PhD thesis, University of Bath.

Retrieved 1 August 2010 from http://www.actionresearch.net/living/ jekan.shtml. JeKan tells how he has come to understand and improve his practice as the only white, male nurse, foreign educator in a culture that is different from his own through learning to understand the educational influences of previous lives as a nurse, educator and Buddhist priest.

2 http://www.jeanmcniff.com
This is Jean McNiff's website. It is also an influential action research website. Here are some examples of academic reports.

Example 1
Chris Glavey (2008) *Helping Eagles Fly: A Living Theory Approach to Student and Young Adult Leadership Development.* PhD thesis, University of Glamorgan.
Retrieved 1 August 2010 from http://www.jeanmcniff.com/items.asp?id=44. Chris explains how he enables young people to overcome their experiences of voicelessness through becoming educational leaders in their own contexts.

Example 2
Ray O'Neill (2007) *ICT as Political Action.* PhD thesis, University of Glamorgan.

Retrieved 1 August 2010 from http://www.ictaspoliticalaction.com/. Ray turns his thesis into a multimedia website, where he explains how he has helped young people appreciate their experiences of learning and using ICT as a form of political action.

REFLECTIVE QUESTIONS

Ask yourself the following questions:

- ✓ Are you clear about the expectations for academic reports?

- ✓ Are you confident that you can write a report that fulfils the expectations?

- ✓ Do you appreciate what the main features of academic writing are in action research?

- ✓ Can you do it? Yes, you can.

SUMMARY

This chapter has set out briefly how to write an academic report. It has outlined the main expectations of academic report writing, and has indicated some of the main features that distinguish an academic report from a workplace-based report.

We now consider how to write a professional portfolio.

Chapter 31
Compiling a professional portfolio

This chapter deals with compiling a professional portfolio, in relation to how you can use an action research approach, and what such a portfolio would look like. It contains the following:

- Issues in compiling a professional portfolio
- Contents of a professional portfolio

ISSUES IN COMPILING A PROFESSIONAL PORTFOLIO

Most practitioners need to compile a professional portfolio at some time, perhaps for a promotion, a new post, or professional appraisal. Given the current emphasis on self-evaluation, action research is an excellent methodology for the job. Here is how you can do it and some specific aspects you need to attend to.

First, keep in mind the idea that action research is a generative transformational methodology, so it is possible to show how one aspect transforms into another, and how the end of one phase becomes the beginning of another.

Also remember that as an action researcher you offer descriptions and explanations for your practice. The descriptions tell what you have done; the explanations tell why you have done it, and what you hope to achieve. Your descriptions and explanations together constitute your living educational theory (Whitehead 1989).

A portfolio is therefore not just a list of activities, but also an explanation for why you have undertaken those activities and what their significance is for your professional learning.

Here is what a professional portfolio looks like.

CONTENTS OF A PROFESSIONAL PORTFOLIO

Take these action steps to compile your professional portfolio.

Step 1
List significant activities over a designated time span

Draw up a list of significant events that you consider important to show what you have done over a particular time period. For example:

2000 Completed Nursing Diploma

2001 Undertook intensive training in psychiatric nursing

2002 Qualified as psychiatric nurse and transferred to psychiatric unit

2005 Undertook management training course

2007 Qualified with Diploma in Nursing Management

2009 Appointed Director of Psychiatric Unit

For each of these activities give a description of what the work involved, how you coped with it, what your experiences were, and so on. This constitutes a descriptive list of what you have done. You can also include any evidence to show the authenticity of what you are saying (see below).

Step 2
Locate the activities within an explanatory framework

The best portfolios embed the activities within an explanatory framework, to show why you did what you did. This gives greater depth to your portfolio, because you show that it is research-based and research-informed.

You can develop your explanatory framework by drawing on the same critical questions as before. Regard compiling your portfolio as you would regard writing a research project.

Here is how you could write your portfolio.

Introduction to the professional portfolio

First write an introduction to tell your reader what they are about to read. Now move into the chapters. Each chapter engages with an action reflection question.

Chapter 1
What is this portfolio about? (What is my concern?)

Say who you are, give your background and contexts, and why you are compiling your portfolio. Say that the portfolio itself represents your knowledge claim, or your original contribution to knowledge of the field, such as enhancing professionalism in your own field of practice (nursing, law, dentistry or management).

Chapter 2
Why have I selected the activities in the portfolio? What do they show? (Why am I concerned? What are my values?)

Give reasons for the selection of activities you have chosen. Say how they show you living your values in your practice. For example, that you have lived a life of caring for other people, or of striving for excellence in leadership.

Chapter 3

What are some of the key aspects of my career? (How do I show the situation as it is, and as it develops?)

List the activities you feel are significant episodes and deserve to go into your professional portfolio. Explain that these episodes act as data for how you have focused on professional development and lifelong learning.

Chapter 4
What do I feel I have achieved? (What were my career options? What did I choose to do?)

Say what you have achieved through your professional career. Say how the activities you describe represent your contribution to your own professional learning and possibly the professional learning of others. Say how you have contributed to improving practice through knowledge production.

Chapter 5
What is special about the episodes I have described? (How do I generate evidence from my data?)

Say what is special about the episodes you have described, in relation to how they represent the living out of your values. Say how you have become a more reflective practitioner, and can demonstrate critical engagement with your own thinking.

Chapter 6

How do I ensure the authenticity of this report? (How do I ensure that any conclusions I come to are reasonably fair and accurate?)

Say that you have tested the validity of the claims you are making against the critical feedback of colleagues and validation groups. Say that the report represents your own self-evaluation, and that your readers themselves will exercise critical judgement in relation to its quality.

Chapter 7

What is the significance of this professional portfolio? (What is the significance of my claims to knowledge?)

Say how doing the work, and compiling this portfolio as an account of the work, is significant for your own professional learning. The work and the portfolio also have the potential to contribute to the professional learning of others, and to enhancing the quality and status of your profession.

Chapter 8

Reflections on the work and the portfolio (How do I modify my ideas and practices in light of my evaluation?)

Say what doing the work, and compiling the portfolio have meant for you. Explain that this portfolio is an account of your professional activity and learning so far, and how the learning from its compilation will inform future work and writing.

EXERCISE

Now draw up your portfolio. Write your own reference for yourself, pointing out your achievements and your learning. Check whether any specific guidelines exist from the person(s) you are writing it for, and ensure that you follow these guidelines – for example, where in the portfolio you should put your certificates, how you should organise the materials, whether you should include appendices ... and so on.

Aim to include as much evidence as possible, to back up your claims to professionalism. Your evidence could include the following:

- Certificates and diplomas
- Testimonials, recommendations and commentaries from colleagues, employers, managers and clients

- Records of achievement
- Photographs and videotapes of yourself in action with others
- Evaluation documents
- Thank you letters
- And so on …

REFLECTIVE QUESTIONS

Here is a checklist for your professional portfolio. Have you:

- ✓ Organised your material in such a way that your reader will see what you have achieved?
- ✓ Located your material within an explanatory framework, so that it is not simply a list of activities?
- ✓ Produced data and evidence to back up any claims?
- ✓ Explained that you have asked for feedback from respected colleagues in relation to the authenticity of what you are saying?
- ✓ Represented yourself fairly and confidently, without appearing arrogant or self-satisfied?

If you have achieved all these things, you have probably produced a portfolio which you can be proud of, and you deserve to get the position you are looking for.

SUMMARY

This chapter has given information on how to compile a professional portfolio. It has emphasised the need to organise any information about yourself within an explanatory framework, so that your professional history does not appear simply as an activities list but as containing explanatory principles that show how you give meaning to your life. You are encouraged especially to ensure that you produce evidence to support any claims you make.

This brings the book to an end. However, the story itself does not end here – the story continues with you.

You should continue with your action enquiry vigorously and with commitment. On the following pages, I explain why I think you should do so.

End word

Thank you for reading this book. I hope you have enjoyed reading it as much as I have enjoyed writing it.

I said on the previous page that I would give my explanations for writing it. Here they are.

First, I believe all people should value themselves, and be valued, for who they are and what they do, not only for what job or responsibilities they hold. I do not agree with equating personal worth with organisational positioning.

Second, in my view all people know what they are doing at a deep level. Perhaps we sometimes go against what we feel is right, but we still know what is right and wrong. Sometimes (in my case at least) we learn as we grow up. Although we may continue to make mistakes, we have a better understanding of what mistakes we are making and why we are making them.

Third, I firmly believe that, pathology aside, all people are capable of thinking for themselves, and offering explanations for those choices. I disagree with the still-dominant messages in the literatures and the media that some people are not able to think for themselves, so others should do their thinking for them. Following ideas from Bateson (1979), and other theorists of environmental evolution, I believe that the living world thinks for itself, and knows what it is doing. It is when people go mad in the world that things start to go wrong. This has far-ranging implications for how we should live within this world.

So, fourth, we live in a world community of increasing intercultural understanding and a recognition that people need to live together for their own survival. This is strongly linked with environmental wellbeing. If we continue quarreling among ourselves about identity, about who knows or is entitled to know, and ravage the earth's resources to fuel those quarrels, we will end up with nothing, and then we will definitely be in trouble, and no amount of knowledge will save us. The beauty of action research is, for me, its emphasis on personal accountability. If each one of us were to accept the responsibility of offering explanations for who we are, how we think, and what we do, the world would become a better place overnight.

For me, therefore, both the troubles of the world and its future salvation lie in our values, logics and epistemologies, and our committing to new personalised forms of knowledge and theory, as outlined in this book: each one of us should account for ourselves by producing our own living educational theories. More to the point, our salvation lies in the underpinning values and logics of non-mainstream epistemologies, and the extent to which we are prepared to commit to thinking for ourselves and our own knowledge-creating capacities.

This is the underpinning philosophy of action research, and it is the philosophy that guides my personal and professional life. If every one of us could resist the temptation of believing everything we are told; learn to think for ourselves and exercise our educational influences in other people's thinking; and show how we hold ourselves accountable for what we are doing – we may find tomorrow that the world is already a better place.

Jean McNiff
Dorset, 11 September 2010

References

Arendt, H. (1994) *Eichmann in Jerusalem: A Report on the Banality of Evil*. New York, Penguin.

Bateson, G. (1979) *Mind and Nature: A Necessary Unity*. New York, Dutton.

Bourdieu, P. (1992) *The Logic of Practice*. Cambridge, Polity.

Corey, S. (1953) *Action Research to Improve School Practices*. New York, Teachers College Press.

Foucault, M. (2001) *Fearless Speech*. Los Angeles, CA, Semiotext(e).

Garnett, J., Costley, C. and Workman, B. (eds) (2009) *Work Based Learning: Journeys to the Core of Higher Education*. Middlesex, Middlesex University Press.

Gibbons, M., Limoges, C., Nowotny, H., Schwartzman, S., Scott, P. and Trow, M. (1994) *The New Production of Knowledge*. London, Sage.

Gould, S.J. (1992) *The Mismeasure of Man*. London, Penguin.

Habermas, J. (1975) *Legitimation Crisis*. Boston, MA, Beacon Press.

Koch, T. and Kralik, D. (2006) *Participatory Action Research in Healthcare*. Oxford, Blackwell.

Kuhn, T. (1964) *The Structure of Scientific Revolutions* (2nd edition). Chicago, University of Chicago Press.

McNiff, J. and Whitehead, J. (2009) *Doing and Writing Action Research*. London, Sage.

McNiff, J. and Whitehead, J. (2010) *You and Your Action Research Project* (3rd edition). Abingdon, Routledge.

McNiff, J. and Whitehead, J. (2011) *All You Need to Know about Action Research* (2nd edition). London, Sage.

Nonaka, I. and Takeuchi, H. (1995) *The Knowledge-Creating Company*. Oxford, Oxford University Press.

Schön, D. (1983) *The Reflective Practitioner: How Professionals Think in Action*. New York, Basic.

Senge, P. (1990) *The Fifth Discipline; The Art and Practice of the Learning Organization*. New York, Doubleday.

Somekh, B. (2006) *Action Research: A Methodology for Change and Development*. Buckingham, Open University Press.

Squire, P. (2009) *How Can a 'Client-Centred' Approach to Selling Lead to the 'Co-Creation' of a New Global Selling Mindset?* PhD Thesis, Middlesex Business School.

Tribal Education UK (2010) (ed. J. McNiff) *Teacher Enquiry Bulletin. Action Research for Teachers in Qatar*. Tribal, London. See also http://www.jeanmcniff.com/qatar.asp

Whitehead, J. (1989) 'Creating a Living Educational Theory from Questions of the Kind, "How Do I Improve my Practice?"', *Cambridge Journal of Education*, 19(1): 137–53.

Index